A man may paint the story of his own adventures on his own tepee. It illuminates his soul and tells the world who he is. But the man who paints fictions is a scoundrel and shunned by the tribe.

American Indian Saying

JOURNEY
TO
MYRTOS:

VIETNAM TO CRETE –
HEALING THE WOUNDS OF WAR

A MEMOIR
By: Robert Mitchell

Book 1 of a Two-Book Memoir:
TAKE THE LONG WAY HOME:
A Vietnam Veteran's 12-Year Odyssey
of Healing and Reintegration

ISBN: 146631303X

ISBN 13: 9781466313033

Library of Congress Control Number: 2011916806
CreateSpace, North Charleston, SC

On the Cover:
Author receives Distinguished Flying Cross
From Maj. General John Tolson, March 1968
Photo by: George Francioni

Contents

Journey To Myrtos: Vietnam To Crete—Healing The Wounds Of War

CHAPTER ONE:

The Goddess
of The Moon

The gods seduce children because children have the imagination and sensitivity to witness their presence. The Goddess of the Moon seduced me when I was eleven years old. I lost her, but then I found her again when I was twenty-five.

In 1957, in the middle of the school year, the engineering firm for which my father worked transferred us from the green suburban hills of the San Francisco peninsula to the earthy and isolated prairie of rural Illinois. We had moved many times before so it was not so much a disruption of my life as it was an opportunity for a new adventure.

I saw our new home for the first time on moving day. Twelve miles from the small town of Morris, where we had been living in a motel, Mother had found a farmhouse to rent. It was the only house in the area large enough for our family. I was the second oldest and the oldest boy of six children.

The narrow asphalt road dipped and forded a shallow creek, then rose slightly and leveled out between vast fields forlorn and barren, dotted with drifts of snow that had been swept up by the wind between furrows bereft of corn. I tuned out the family chatter in the car and the hum of the engine and listened to the lonely sound of the cold gusts of wind that whistled over the broken stalks in low, muted tones that repelled the timid and called to the bold in a ghostly whisper that resonated like the soft, mellow sound of a cello.

We turned onto a gravel driveway that crossed a wooden bridge over a drainage ditch and ran up the side of the lawn beyond the house to the barn. The two-story frame house, built early in the century, sat back from the road on a stone foundation. Its roof gables pointed to the four directions and a broad-roofed porch stretched across its front. There were enough bedrooms so that, for the first time, I could have my own room. I ran up and down the stairs exploring the house from the basement, with its coal-fired furnace, coal bin and cool dark cistern for storing well water to the empty attic, with its unobstructed view through the gable windows. I stood looking out over a vast, open landscape that called me away from the suburban life we had left behind in San Francisco.

The winter snow melted. Spring blossomed, and the squishy earth under my feet smelled of dampness and manure. Air currents, made visible by dust devils that danced on the wind, carried flocks of black-birds that noisily called to me as they dipped and swirled, surfing the invisible waves that plied between the shifting clouds and the fresh plowed fields.

That spring, a neighboring farmer leased and worked the land. He was like a grandfather, letting me ride the tractor with him when he plowed the fields. I wondered if the owner of the property had died or just abandoned the farm to move to the city. Now we rented the house and someone else worked the land. It was a farm without a farmer, and I sensed the loneliness of a property without a master. That feeling deepened the bond between the Illinois prairie and me.

Spring turned to summer. School was out. I liked being alone, out in the country, and I used my imagination to invent new adventures. My brother, Bill, and I explored the area on our bikes, but that got boring because the land was all flat and the cornfields were all the same. Then I found a refuge in the barn, where I could be alone.

At first, I felt small standing in the enormous space that had the damp smell of musty hay and a voice of creaking timbers and shallow whistles where the wind blew through the broken boards in the walls. The animal pens and hayloft were intact, but the huge space was emp-ty, except for the mice I could hear scurrying around, and a barn owl that slept in the rafters. The mysterious sounds she made frightened me, until I spotted her globular eyes gazing down from the shadows and realized what was making the noise. After a while, we grew used to each other, and she greeted me and followed my movements each time I entered the barn.

I found a warm, sunny spot behind the barn that was accessible through a hidden hole in the wall, behind a board that hung on a nail in the back of one of the animal pens. Several rows of fences and pens around the backside of the barn kept my secret place isolated from the house, so my siblings did not disturb me. Sometimes, I took a book out there to read. But some days the warmth of the sun seduced me. I leaned back against the wall, just feeling the heat on my clothes. Then I took off my shirt, opened my pants and masturbated to fantasies heightened by the warmth of the sun on my bare skin.

I had no such freedom when we lived in the suburbs. But from the moment we moved to the farm I knew that I was free from the social restraints of living in town. Here, our nearest neighbor was a mile away.

Except for the huge front lawn that Bill and I had to mow, our house and barn were surrounded by rows and rows of corn ripening in the sun. The long narrow leaves on stalks crowned with golden tassels danced in the wind and gave the landscape the appearance of a rippling sea of green that waved in the summer breezes all around our rectangular island in a sea of corn.

For many families in the 1950s, evenings together were typically defined by the glow of the television set. Out on the farm, we had to entertain ourselves. We had a television, but it didn't work very well in the country.

After supper, Mother sat in a rocking chair on the porch with my baby sister on her lap. Dad sat on the front steps, alternately discussing the events of his workday with her and watching the five of us. With my two brothers and my two other sisters, I chased fireflies. We caught them in our hands and placed them in Mason jars that hung on the ends of sticks like Japanese lanterns. The evening deepened, and we marveled at the arc of the Milky Way that was remarkably visible against the blackness of a night sky un-polluted by city lights. Dad named some of the constellations, but the one that I remembered was *Orion,* because I could always find the three stars that made up his belt.

When we had released the fireflies and the three little children had been put to bed, my older sister, Pat, my brother Bill and I sat on the living room floor in our pajamas while Dad read us stories and fairytales from one of the *Childcraft* books that were always kept in our living room. Then he ushered us up to our rooms and tucked us in.

Alone, in the quiet of the night, I lay awake in my bed, and my imagination—triggered by one of Dad's stories or the whisper of a passing thought—filled me with wondrous visions as I slowly drifted off to sleep.

Then, in the darkest hours when all were asleep and the house was quiet, I awoke to a soft whisper calling me, drawing me under the cover of darkness, into the night. For a long time I lay in my bed, measuring the muted sounds of my sleeping family and listening to the seductive voice that had awakened me from my dream-space.

I slipped out of my bed, out of my room and down the stairs. I opened the front door and stood on the porch barefoot in my pajamas, surrendering myself to the spirit that had called me there.

The moon cast a silvery glow, though it was already descending toward the western horizon. The sky sparkled with the powdery filament of a million stars of the Milky Way, like a jeweled veil against the velvety black bosom of the night. A warm breeze rustled the broad leaves of the regal corn stalks at the edge of the field, only fifty feet away.

Slowly, I unbuttoned the shirt of my pajamas. I felt the caress of warm breezes, while the light cotton shirt flapped behind me. I listened for movement in the house, and when I was sure that everyone was still asleep, I descended the steps, placing my bare feet carefully on the treads so as not to make the boards squeak. At the foot of the steps, I turned and looked up at the dark silhouette of the house framed by the glow of the setting moon. A light, warm breeze caressed the nape of my neck. I slipped off my pajama shirt and hung it on the balustrade. Then, before the thought of an inhibition could enter my head, I slipped off my pajama pants and stood naked on the lawn.

A powerful new freedom, greater than I had ever known living in the suburbs, washed over me. I walked into the cornfield, feeling the plowed earth squishing up between my toes. A wind whispered through the stalks that towered above my head, twisting the leaves that danced for me and welcomed me into their presence. I pulled the silky tassels of the corn down so that they draped over my body and caressed me. And I offered myself to the Goddess of the Moon.

Guided by an inner spirit and directed by the unseen music of the night, I danced. I moved my body with tenderness and gesture among the rows and stalks of corn, feeling their leaves and tassels brush against my skin. I knew, as I danced among the delicate veils of moonlight, that the goddess was watching. It was like making love to nature in the presence of the gods.

☆ ☆ ☆

Worship of the Goddess of the Moon was really a part of my family heritage. My mother's mother was a Moon, the daughter of Dr. William Henry Moon, an early Alabama pioneer. During that summer on the farm, my mother's sister, Aunt Francine, came to visit. She had studied the family genealogy and, because she was an actress, she loved to tell stories.

Her arms and hands flailed in the air and she pulled one of those actor-masks over her face as she told us stories of our ancestors that had come from Normandy and England. Once, a long, long time ago, she said, they had been druids. They cut mistletoe from the oak trees in the forest with golden sickles to make the potion for their ceremonies, where they danced for the Goddess of the Moon. Francine said the Moons got that name because they were all druids.

Then, while Pat, Bill and I sat under the spell of Francine's dramatic presentation, Mother and Francine burst into giggles until we were all rolling on the floor with laughter. But at night, when the world was still, the spirits of those ancestors called to me as one of their own.

In the sixteen hundreds, the Moons crossed the Atlantic and settled in Virginia. My great, great grandfather moved first to Georgia and then to Alabama, and his son, my great grandfather, William Henry Moon, was a decorated Confederate soldier in the Civil War. My grandmother was the sixth of his eleven children.

I never knew my grandmother because she died of Leukemia when my mother was only fourteen. My mother—the third of six children—carried the Moon legacy. She took over raising her three younger

5

siblings until my grandfather remarried. Like the Goddess of the Moon she was a caring and nurturing woman and a good mother.

✫ ✫ ✫

Her domain was the kitchen at the back of the house that looked out toward the barn. In spite of having six children, Mother remained pretty and slender. She always wore dresses or long skirts with low heeled shoes, smelled of some favorite musty-rose perfume and wore her hair, neither long nor short, in a stylish, 1950s permanent.

In the kitchen, she moved with grace from the sink to the refrigerator where she crouched low, searching for the ingredients of the evening meal—the light from the appliance surrounding her in a shimmering halo. Her long slender hands glistened with moisture as they flowed from the sink to the counter, skinning and washing the pieces of chicken she was about to fry.

I always felt like I was her favorite, and I often helped in the kitchen. I peeled potatoes and stood near by, simply watching her and feeling her presence, for mostly our relationship consisted of a special sense and mood rather than words. I felt at peace in her presence and loved being with her, helping in the kitchen and helping with the babies, who sat in high chairs.

While she worked, Mother often hummed or sang softly in the smooth alto voice that on Sunday mornings graced the church choir. Then, when one of the girls made an uncomfortable sound, Mother directed me, "Bobby, see what's making the baby cry." She spoke in a smooth Alabama drawl that revealed the antebellum aristocracy of her family and the small Alabama town where she had been raised, and where I had been born.

By embracing my mother's world, I found refuge from the sterner discipline of my father. As a professional civil engineer, Dad had developed the rational, controlled side of his own nature and, it seemed, he wanted me to follow in his footsteps. At the age of eleven, I didn't really understand his pragmatic expectations of me, but I did understand that those expectations were a threat to my imaginative way of looking at the world. It clashed with my sensitivities and drove me to my mother's side.

☆ ☆ ☆

Dad had been assigned to the main offices of the Bechtel Corporation in San Francisco, where he directed the cost analysis and bidding on the nation's first commercial Nuclear Power Plant—to be built on Dresden Island in the Illinois River, about fifty miles from Chicago. When Bechtel won the bid, we were sent to Illinois where Dad was the chief construction engineer on the project. The farmhouse where we lived was about ten miles away.

But Dad was too independent to be a good corporate man. In the fall, only eight months after we had moved to Illinois, he had an irreconcilable conflict with the corporate Project Manager, and Bechtel executives in San Francisco threatened to move our family once again. Dad rebelled against the dictates of far-off overseers and began searching for a different and more stable job in Chicago. We moved from the cornfields of the open prairie to the quiet, upscale suburb of River Forest, into a small house on Chicago Avenue. Like all our moves following Dad's building projects, I simply took this one in stride. Anyway, I told myself, winter on the farm would not have been much fun.

In the house on Chicago Avenue, I shared a large bedroom with both of my brothers. The room had access, through a screened-in porch, to a long, fenced-in corner yard of trees and shrubs that bordered on the avenue. Often, as I had done the year before, on sweltering summer nights I awoke to a whispered allure of the night wind.

At first, I was intimidated by my brothers sleeping so close to me and by the crowded suburban setting that was so different from the lonely isolation of the house in the cornfield, but I could not resist the call. I slipped out of my bed and went to the porch, where I stood shirtless, allowing myself to be caressed by the night breeze, while watching to see how many cars passed along the avenue at that late hour. Then a light, warm breeze caressed the hairs on the nape of my neck, and I knew it was a signal that the spirits of the night were summoning me.

I grew bold, stripped off my pajama pants and went out into the yard naked—darting from the cover of the car parked in the driveway to the shadows cast by nearby shrubs. I moved from tree to tree toward the far corner of the lot and as far as possible from the house, my senses heightened to avoid detection by the occupants of a passing car or a lonely pedestrian out for a night stroll or my father going to the kitchen for a glass of water. Again, in the solitude of a pagan ritual, I communed with both the world of nature and the realm of the spirits. I felt the cool earth under my bare feet, let the leaves of bushes brush against my body, hugged the trunks of trees and climbed up into the branches where I crouched naked and silently mimicked howling at the moon. In the darkness of the suburban night, all my senses were alert, my soul alive, my imagination searching the ether for the faces of those spirits of my ancestors: the druid Moons, who spoke with the goddess. But still their faces remained hidden in the shadows.

More than just the setting was different from the year before. I was a year older and a year more self-conscious. I was a year closer to knowing that my actions defied the social conventions and unseen authors of the rigid expectations imposed on boys my age. In the daylight, at school I was expected to conform to the social conventions defined by our upper middle class suburban life and to be like the other kids. But in the shadows of the night I rebelled against the mask of civility that I was expected to wear in the daylight—the mask worn by my classmates and friends; the mask that would grow into the model of modern manhood that I was expected to become. Thus, my rebellion was directed against the sensible social behavior and pragmatic logic represented by the authority of my father.

Not that Dad's demands were exceedingly harsh; they were not. As chief engineer on various projects building segments of the Eisenhower and Dan Ryan Expressways in Chicago, he had a demanding job and, like so many fathers, left the day-to-day raising of his children to Mother. Yet he still represented all the rational vigilance and strict behavioral demands placed on the raising of boys. The long rod of his discipline stung my butt when I defied those demands or when he coerced me toward a stringent self-vigilance with the admonition, "For crying-out-loud, Bobby, act your age!"

But to me his command was vague. It did not specify how acting my age differed from running around naked in the yard communing with the night wind and looking for my inner spirit mirrored in the faces of my ancestors. Then, in a twist of mood, he would commend me for the diligence with which I performed my household chores or the perseverance that led to getting a good grade on a school test. Thus I found his expectations confusing.

I didn't really understand the model of modern manhood he was holding before me, and that model remained an un-decipherable mystery. So I clung tenaciously to the illusive spirits of my mother's ancestors and my fading memory of the ritual in the cornfield. I clung to the hope that they would unlock the secret of my "true" identity and clarify my destiny.

Perhaps my mother sensed the affinity I had for communing with the spirits of nature—an affinity that, after all, I had inherited from her: from the legacy of the Moons. In that sense, in the twilight years of my childhood, she still provided a refuge for my sensitive nature, which was trying to find a way to express itself. She was my comfort. At a time when it was expected that I should break free of my mother's apron strings to embrace the world of my father and society, I clung more closely to her.

It was during the year when I was wrestling with those conflicting emotions that we discovered that Mother had breast cancer. Only then did I learn that she had already had her first mastectomy as a teenager, several years after her mother had died of Leukemia.

In the spring of her thirty-eighth year, Mother entered the hospital for her second mastectomy. The operation appeared to be successful, and she seemed to respond well to chemotherapy and radiation treatments. Our family life was made more difficult by the demands and expenses of her illness, but for most of the following year, she seemed to be getting better and our lives remained fairly normal. Then, during the second year of her illness, it was discovered that the cancer was spreading. Relapses sent her back to the hospital for more operations and more treatments.

We moved from the house on Chicago Avenue to a much larger house several blocks away. During the fall, mother returned home from an extensive hospital stay. Our new house had a large master bedroom, part of which was outfitted with a rented hospital bed. There was a large bedside table with a tray full of medications and a walker and wheelchair stood nearby so that Mother could move around. While this antiseptic setting was now set up in our home, my brothers and sisters and I clung to Mother and continued to believe that soon she would be back to her normal self.

Then, late one night, I suddenly awoke. I was lying in that state of half-slumber where the spirits are most active, but I did not sense the quiet allure of the night wind or whispers from the spirits of my ancestors. At that moment, a great sadness came over me. An emotional sigh emanated from the core of my being, causing my chest to quiver uncontrollably and gripping my heart so tightly that, for an instant, it stopped—fearful that another beat would arouse the attention of the dark spirit that had entered the room.

I knew then that my mother would die. The knowledge did not come as a premonition evolving from an unanswered question, or from a mere belief. No. It was an incontestable truth carried on the wings of a Messenger of Death and deposited on the doorstep of my consciousness. A deep sense of hopelessness overcame me. I tried to squeeze tears from my soul, but I could not cry. Unable to share my deep intuition with anyone, it felt as if a secret truth had been given to me to keep—a warning from the spirits of my ancestors that everything in my life was about to change.

A couple of weeks before Christmas, just before dawn, we were suddenly awakened by a terrifying scream of pain that shook the whole house. Mother had fallen from her hospital bed and broken her hip. My two little sisters cried in terror. Dad called the doctor and an ambulance. He directed my sister, Pat, to look after the two little girls and see to it that our two brothers got off to school. Then, he turned to me and said

I was to accompany Mother to the hospital in the ambulance while he followed in the car.

I held her hand, not so much to comfort her, for she was drugged with painkillers and barely conscious, but to convey with that physical gesture the special bond that I had always felt existed between us. That bond had become more intense as I explored my inner sensitivities under the guidance of a vague but now familiar feminine deity that, in a mysterious way, was the family legacy that my mother carried with her. It was the very essence of my mother's soul—the very essence of my soul.

Then she opened her eyes. She could not speak, but she looked at me as though to warn me to prepare myself for her death. I was fourteen, and the years of my adolescence still lay before me. I was vulnerable and frightened, for she was, to me, my only link to the illusive inner spirit that would define and guide me, and she was dying.

Yet too, I somehow knew that she was cautioning me not to be defeated, not to become a participant in my own self-estrangement. She was telling me that she understood me, but that she could no longer be my refuge. She would not be there to comfort my growing pains or temper the feelings that smoldered beneath the façade of my emerging adolescent ego. She could not nurture the side of my personality that needed to lift the veil of the rational and the sensible and peek beneath the logical world of my father to reveal the ancient spirits that lurked there. She would have done that because she too sensed the presence of those spirits and I knew that she sensed them in me. Now, though I was unprepared to accept her warning and all that it implied about the forces that would shape my life after she was gone, she was letting go, breaking the bond between mother and son that had to be broken.

For six months she clung to life. Dad's mother came to Chicago to take care of the house and the six of us, while he spent his evening hours after work at her side. Mother's last words to him were, "Honey, I just can't leave you with all those children to raise." But in June of 1960, my mother died.

CHAPTER TWO:

The Warlords
of the Patriarchy

At the age of fourteen, I did not know what the patriarchy was, but still it was about to take over my life and define my destiny. My adolescent years were spiritually void and characterized by the Sisyphean task of rolling the great boulder of my sorrow to the top of the mountain, only to have it roll back again, crushing me beneath its interminable weight.

Still, I did not blame God for Mother's death. Both my brother Bill and our younger brother, perhaps as a way of understanding her death, eventually found religion and became lifelong followers of the church—a conversion that took place for them at the age of eleven or twelve, about the same age that I began communing with the Goddess of the Moon. I did not have a Christian epiphany. Of course I attended church services, listened to the sermons and was a member of the Methodist Youth Fellowship. But the stern and distant Father, Yahweh, did not come down into our Fellowship Hall to dance with us, the way the Goddess of the Moon had invited me to dance in the cornfield. The spirits of my ancestors had introduced me to the goddess, and that was how I experienced my epiphany. I simply knew that I was more a son of the goddess than of the Father.

Still, as my memory of my mother began to fade the memory of my spiritual awakening faded as well. I met the challenges of grow-ing up with bold determination, but success—defined either in terms of completing my initiation into selfhood with the help of the spirits of my ancestors, or in meeting the social expectations of the middle class—eluded me.

Even though it conflicted with the sensitivity of my true nature, the rational, pragmatic values, so prized by my father, came more and more to define my character. It was just easier to let rationalizations overshadow my feelings—the same rationalizations that my father used when he explained that the tear glands of adult males dry-up, so that men cannot cry. Subsequently, I kept my emotions hidden behind a mask of seriousness.

At school I surrendered to the social group. Much of the day-to-day routine—the way boys related to each other, to academics, to extra-curricular activities and to girls—seemed to support an emotionally detached model of modern manhood, and that was the persona that began to define me. At home, I simply surrendered to my father's expectations, suppressing my irrational emotions and my grief, and containing my sorrow over the loss of my mother so that it would not overcome me.

Dad was forced to wear a mask of resolute strength by the need to keep his job and hold his family together. Still, Mother's death took a tragic toll on him as a parent. My grandmother took the two little girls to be raised by my father's brother and his wife in California. Then, the paternal warmth that Mother had so easily evoked and that laid just beneath his pragmatic exterior turned frigid.

Dad became morose and found his solace in alcohol and television. After supper he would stand in the back of the living room with a blank stare on his face, sipping bourbon, unresponsive to the flickering lights of the television as it rolled seamlessly into the canned entertainment and laughter of the *Tonight Show*. Though he remained an intelligent and competent engineer and took good care of his children, the alcohol had the effect of burying his role as an emotionally warm parent deeper beneath a resolute and pragmatic mask of insensitivity. My primary model of modern manhood became emotionally distant and completely inaccessible.

Still, from that moment in the ambulance when my mother's legacy was cemented to my soul, my defiance of the expectations of my father and the patriarchy he represented was kept smoldering deep down inside. Outwardly, I was compelled even by my peers to repress those feelings. Though when I awoke in the middle of the night, I quietly grieved for my mother. Still, calling out to the feminine spirit that evoked my deepest and most mysterious sensitivities was only met with silence.

☆ ☆ ☆

I graduated from high school in 1963 and attended the University of Illinois at Urbana, where I studied architecture. Conceding to Dad's expectations rather than my own enthusiasm, I pledged the Alpha Tau Omega fraternity, because Dad had been an ATO. I also joined the Naval ROTC (Reserve Officer Training Corps), because it was required of all incoming male students and because Dad had served in the Navy as an aircraft maintenance officer in World War II.

It only took one semester for me to realize that I was uneasy with life as a full-time student in the strange, new environment of the university. Since I was enthusiastic about design, one of my deepest expectations was to find a mentor who would take a personal interest in me and help guide me through my professional studies, but I did not find an inspiring teacher. Neither did I find a fraternity brother with whom I could develop a meaningful, one-on-one relationship to replace the two close friends with whom I had attended junior high and high school and who were now attending distant colleges. I was alone—not with the freedom of my solitude, but alone in the midst of a dynamic and competitive world that demanded compliance.

During my third semester, I became increasingly uncomfortable with a university social life centered on drinking, and that led me deeper into a sense of social isolation. I failed a class, flunked out of the university, moved back home, enrolled in a correspondence course to make up the course I had failed and found a job as a draftsman in the engineering division of the Sunbeam Corporation. Though I was relieved to be away from the life of a full-time student in Urbana, my father believed that I was just drifting—and told me so. But his admonition fell on deft ears, because I already knew that he was incapable of empathizing with my deep emotional turmoil. I was torn between an inner spirit that was falling deeper into the shadows and the pressure to live up to a vague model of modern manhood devoid of spirituality.

☆ ☆ ☆

In the summer of 1965, tired of doing mechanical drawings of Sunbeam toasters and blenders, I went looking for a job with an architect, striving to get back on a sensible career path that led between two minefields: my wounded sensitivities and the opaque but persistent expectations of my father's world that weighed so heavily on my soul. I was fortunate to find a job with Albert Ramp—an architectural firm of one architect.

Al fell as easily into the master-apprentice relationship as I did and involved me in all of the phases of the work, from surveying the property, to tutoring me on the order and layout of each page of the working drawings. Together, we revisited the job sites on regular inspection tours.

After one such visit, on the way back to the office, Al began to lament nostalgically. "The old craftsmen are dying off," he said. "Apprenticeships in the crafts are a thing of the past. There just aren't any young artisans to take their place." Al continued talking about how hard it was to find good masons who could do artistic brickwork. "And if you want really nice tile," he said, "it has to be imported from Mexico or Morocco." Decorative plaster, like the artistic friezes that corniced the ceilings of many older, classic buildings, had been replaced with quick, cheap plaster or drywall. Furthermore, Al remarked, when you could find the craftsmen to do the work, it was expensive, and the client was always attentive to the bottom line.

Al's ruminations were just conversation but, like a splash of cold water, they had the effect of waking me from a romantically tinted dream, and some of the realities of being an architect began to sink in. Economics ruled the profession. The sudden realization that my creativity as an architect would always be compromised by factors over which I had no control gave me pause to reconsider the career decision I had made at the age of fourteen, when I was looking desperately for a refuge for my sensitive spirit. I found it in the creative work of building, and I became infatuated with the prairie homes of Frank Lloyd Wright that were so prominent in the Chicago suburbs of River Forest and Oak Park where we lived.

But too, I was now set on a secure career course that would meet all the expectations of my upbringing. It would leave me well situated in a small architectural firm with a loyal clientele and traditional roots in the foundations of Chicago's prestigious architectural heritage. After a few years, I could get married, have kids, join the Rotary Club, be successful and, perhaps, even inherit the firm when Al retired.

But then that anguished voice deep down inside me cried, "WAIT!" Was there to be no awakening of my soul? No initiation in which the face of my inner spirit would reveal itself to guide me? No coming-of-age adventure, just a relatively smooth transition from adolescence to a career? That was the pathway that lay before me, yet, my inner spirit warned: *Be wary of complacency—that dark shadow that covers the soul like a warm blanket and makes you snuggle closer into the bed that you have made for yourself in which you lie sleeping, only dreaming of life's adventures.*

Still, I knew that, for my father, my graduation from college would be my symbolic coming-of-age. I stifled my inner voice and, in the fall, returned to college. The reason that my ever-pragmatic father was so concerned was that full-time college students were exempt from the military draft.

Following the Gulf of Tonkin incident in August of 1964, in which North Vietnamese patrol boats attacked a US naval vessel, Congress gave President Johnson unrestricted power to wage war in Vietnam. Dad supported the effort but was concerned because both Bill and I were old enough to be drafted.

I settled into a comfortable schedule of working full-time for Al Ramp during the day but, in order to keep my 2-S student deferment status, I began taking a full load of college courses in the evening. The liberal arts courses that I took broadened my horizons, but they did not fulfill college credit requirements for my architectural license—a detail that did not go un-remarked by my father.

✳ ✳ ✳

In spite of what, for me, had been a shallow social experience at the University of Illinois I had made one new friend, Carl, and we remained close friends after I left the university. Carl and I had met at the end of my first semester, on the day that I left the fraternity house and moved into the independent residence hall. As I carried a load of my things up to my room, I saw him standing at the end of the hallway, gazing out of the window. The sunlight caught his blond curls, refracting a golden aura around his head. As I walked down the hall toward my room, he transformed from a dark statue, framed by the outside light, into a living being. It was obvious that he had just come in from a run, as he was still dressed in his running shoes, gym pants and a sweaty tank top. He was wiping the sweat from his brow with the loose sleeve of the hooded sweatshirt that was draped over his shoulders.

I didn't know if he had seen me, but I felt obliged to give some kind of greeting. I offered a single word, "Hey," acknowledging his presence but not revealing the fact that I had spent the long patient moments of my walk down the empty hall staring at him. He looked melancholy and lonely. After my semester in the fraternity house, I was lonely too. Carl turned and looked at me. Then, his face lit up with something between a casual smile and a grin. "You must be the new guy. We're right across the hall from each other. Need some help?"

Carl's good looks and congenial personality would have made him popular in any school. In high school he had been a popular jock, play-ing soccer and winning awards in track. But most of his high school friends did not attend college, or had drifted away, leaving Carl more lonely than he would have admitted and, perhaps, just as ill at ease on the university campus as I was.

During the following year, our friendship deepened. He was a year older than me and fell into playing the role of my "older brother," a kind of mentor. I did look up to him. Carl was a dynamic extrovert who car-ried the attributes prized by the patriarchy that I felt were the failures in my own character. In spite of that difference, we both needed to share the transition from dependence on our fathers to that of a soul free to choose its own bonds. What was clear, as our friendship grew, was that neither one of us wanted to make that leap alone.

Though we were both at an age when many young men become committed to a woman, neither of us was ready for that kind of intense relationship. I had a semi-steady girlfriend at the university, but it was not a serious commitment and "casual" sex—like it had been in high school—was burdened with all the pre-liberation baggage epitomized by male chauvinist sexism and the nice-girls-don't-do-it syndrome. She was a nice girl. We went on dates and made-out, but then I went home to masturbate.

Handsome, athletic, charming and outgoing, Carl didn't need a steady girlfriend. Casual sex was not a problem, and whenever he needed a girl, he just picked one up. He had the *knack*. I didn't know what the "knack" was, but I knew I didn't have it. Still, that quality of Carl's character and my own growing indifference to developing a serious relationship with a woman meant that we didn't delude each other with inflated stories of our "conquests" or prattle over the frustration of trying to pick up girls.

After I left the university to move back to Oak Park, I sometimes drove the 200 miles to Urbana on Friday so we could spend the weekend together. Though Dad had met Carl, he never inquired about him the way he often inquired about my high school friends who were attending distant colleges. I sensed that he did not like this developing new friendship. Perhaps he felt that Carl's free-spirited attitude about life would distract me from the pragmatic course I had set for myself. When Carl came home for weekends or vacations, I just told Dad that I would be spending the weekend with Carl at his parent's house in Naperville, a half-hour drive from Oak Park.

Carl's parents had emigrated from Germany in the early 1930s and both accepted me in their home with all the sincerity and hospitality so evident of Old World charm. With a much older brother and two older, married sisters, Carl was the baby of the family. "A hole in the rubber. My parent's little mistake," he called himself, with a little chuckle of self-depredation that revealed how deeply he felt that the little joke-phrases he coined to describe himself might have held a hint of truth, adding another shade of melancholy to his lonely soul. When his parents took me into their home, I sensed that the warm, heartfelt affection that they showed for me grew out of their deep relief that, after two isolated years in the university, Carl had finally found a special friendship to dispel the loneliness that they could feel in him but could do nothing to fill.

At the university, Carl had a double major in Business and German language studies, but he was also a ranking cadet commander in the Army ROTC. The military was the real focus of Carl's career ambition. I had overcome my own flirtation with the military after my stint in the Naval ROTC, though concerns about military service, represented by the threat of getting caught up in the war in Vietnam, loomed over the heads of all of us who were in our late teens and early twenties in 1966. But Carl looked forward to being in the war. He was serious and proud of his military stature and carried himself well in his olive-drab uniform with the gold and black insignias of leadership. His poised command posture, his style and his spirit made Carl very much the model of a modern young warrior. That heroic, warrior spirit was so much a part of his character that he would not allow me or a steady girlfriend or anything else to come between him and his pursuit of a military career. That obsession, it seemed, grew out of his undisguised ambition to follow in the footsteps of his older brother, Paul.

Twelve years Carl's senior, Paul was a graduate of West Point. He was already a field-grade army officer and a rising star in the command structure of a re-invigorated military that, a dozen years after the Korean War, was well on its way to another major war to contain communist aggression in Asia. Paul was looking forward to combat in the military's escalating counter-insurgency war in Vietnam. That same future as a warrior loomed before Carl.

But he was also well aware that the summer of 1966 would be his last opportunity to dispel the restiveness of youth before he graduated from the university the following January, received his commission in the Army and shouldered the responsibilities of modern manhood. Our mutual affection stirred my restless inner spirit back to life, a spirit that for so long had been stifled by my father's insensitivity and the imperious expectations of the patriarchy. Our friendship revived me from the seriousness and isolation of my adolescence and set me free, again. Carl re-awakened my sense of adventure that was slowly dying with my mother's death, my father's unreasonable expectations, my dissatisfaction with the university and my disillusionment with my career.

We planned an adventure to spend the summer of 1966 in Germany. Carl secretly corresponded with an aunt who had a business in a small village near Stuttgart and who surreptitiously agreed to hire us for part of the summer. We were saving money for the airfare. As April rolled into May, I could no longer keep the secret, for I had to ask Al Ramp to let me take the summer off. Business had slowed, and Al agreed to let me take a ten-week leave of absence from my architectural apprenticeship. Also, I had to find a way to inform my father of our decision.

"No! You are not going to go to Germany," was his unusually stern and decisive reaction. It was the only occasion when Carl's father and my father talked with each other, but they were both in agreement on their decision to squash our plans for the Germany trip. Though perhaps my father would have preferred that I stayed home and worked, Carl's father still understood the importance of allowing his son the pleasure of the last summer of his youth. He also understood that it was important for Carl to have a special friend with whom to share it. Letting us have the family's summer cabin on Spider Lake in northern Wisconsin for the summer was our consolation prize.

That summer brought back some of the joys of adolescence that I had missed growing up in Oak Park—a sense of a shared adventure with someone my own age that was free from the expectations of adult authorities that had already been dulled by domestication. For a brief moment, I had another glimpse at that lost sensitivity that gave me access to my inner spirit.

In August, when I arrived back home, my notice from the military Draft Board was waiting—anxiously noted by my father but unopened. It said that my draft status had been reclassified from 2-S, a student deferment, to 1-A, an eminent draft choice. How could that have happened? I had registered for another full-load of evening classes in the fall, and I had made the proper arrangements for my student deferment papers. Somebody had screwed up, but it wasn't me.

I suppose if I hadn't been so intent on a summer fling—if I had stayed home and attended to my job, as my father would have preferred—I would have been in a position to nip this little mistake in the bud. Nothing dramatic, just a few anxious days while I cleared up the paperwork and had my student deferment reinstated. But now, there was a new twist. Was this the pathway Fate opened for me, and for which I had been waiting all my life?

No! I had no ambition to join the military. I had played along with Carl because I knew that he was psychologically preparing himself for his career, but I wasn't so naïve as to get dragged into a foreign adventure of the warlords of the American patriarchy. I could not relate to Carl's ambition to command, nor did I want to go to Vietnam to fight a war for which I had no patriotic enthusiasm. The summer had opened up a whole new vista of possibilities for me. Though my career path was uncertain and the direction my rediscovered spirit of adventure would take was not yet determined, I had no intention of becoming a soldier. I shoved the changes in my draft status into the denial drawer in the back of my mind and returned to my job with Al Ramp. I completed my registration at the college and began evening classes as scheduled.

But in September, I turned twenty-one. As it turned out, my coming-of-age as an adult in modern American society had been predetermined all along. Seamlessly, I accepted my new status as an adult and the conviction that it was up to me to take the initiative in finding my own direction. The draft could not be ignored. The build-up of the war in Vietnam, reported nightly on the evening news, was too intense. But neither was I going to allow myself to be drafted into the army as a foot soldier—cannon fodder for the war machine.

A few days after my birthday, without consulting my father, I went to the local recruitment center and took the qualifying exam for army flight school. A few days after that, I was informed that I had been accepted as a WORWAC, a Warrant Officer Rotary Wing Aviation Cadet. I was going to become a helicopter pilot in the Vietnam War.

Since my days in the ROTC, I had wanted to learn to fly. The army was looking for young men to train as helicopter pilots. A Warrant Officer was not a command position, but neither was it a position as a rank and file soldier. Helicopter pilots were designated specialists and appointed—by warrant of the president—to officer rank with all of the pay and prestige of the officer corps. Too, this was a real adventure and, perhaps, just the nourishment I needed to feed my reawakening inner spirit.

Once I became enthusiastic, the prospect of this new adventure went far beyond any influence that Carl might have had. To me, it seemed as though the warlords of the patriarchy had opened an unexpected pathway toward my initiation into selfhood. Suddenly, the possibility of completing the process that had begun in an Illinois cornfield ten years before, and finally seeing the face of my inner guiding spirit, loomed before me, and I intended to take advantage of it. I was about to embark on the most exhilarating initiation adventure of impending manhood: WAR!

CHAPTER THREE:

The Warrior Spirit

The army treated its prize recruits much better than draftees. At Chicago's Union Station, I boarded a train called the *City of New Orleans* and left for basic training camp at Fort Polk, Louisiana. I was given a voucher for dinner in the dining car and a private sleeping berth for the night. Early the next morning, awakened by the conductor, I left that train in Yazoo City, Mississippi, transferred to a slow moving milk-train to Shreveport, Louisiana and then another transfer to Leesville, home of Fort Polk.

It was a mild January day in the south, and I spent most of the train ride leaning out of the window, contemplating the gravity of my decision. I was confronted with a dilemma that, I suppose, arose from the youthful perspective of egotistical self-importance that the big events in life must come either from willful decisions or uncontrollable circumstances. But it occurred to me that, while my decision was not entirely motivated by circumstances of my own choosing, neither did I feel like I was just a victim of the times. That was the dilemma.

I adopted a fatalistic outlook, concluding that, for reasons still unknown to me, my inner spirit had purposely driven me toward this new adventure. When Fate came knocking, I opened the door and surrendered myself not to the warlords of the patriarchy but to Fate.

I had to prepare myself for the role Fate wanted me to play, and I turned my attention to the war. To fight the counter-insurgency, the army had reorganized into airmobile combat units. Troop transport by helicopter was supported by supply operations and by helicopters outfitted as gunships, medical evacuation ships, scout ships and airborne command-and-control platforms. Helicopters inserted infantry troops into a small area, which they secured by means of search-and-destroy missions. When the job was done, the soldiers were extracted by helicopter.

That unconventional pattern was repeated over and over in Vietnam, and both the commanders on the ground and the politicians in Washington were escalating the war toward a decisive victory. Escalation meant an increased refinement of the concept of helicopter warfare, and training replacement pilots had become one of the highest priorities of the war. Being part of that effort gave me an elitist sense of pride in the role that I would play.

When my train arrived at Leesville station, a sergeant from the base was waiting for me. Three other recruits had arrived on an earlier train and stood at ease in a line on the platform in front of the station house, waiting for me to join them. I quickly sized up my fellow recruits. John was a good-looking guy who wore a smirk on his face that smacked of defiance of military authority. Bob looked distant and arrogant. Mike was a slender youth, with sad eyes and a melancholy look.

I fell into line with them. The sergeant said "Attention!" We straightened our backs, looked straight ahead and tried not to giggle at the silliness we felt in assuming the unaccustomed posture. The sergeant said a few forgettable words—a well-rehearsed and oft-spoken speech about our induction into the army, delivered without emotion and without acknowledging us as individuals. Then, he said, "Left face!" We turned and marched to a waiting vehicle, and he drove us to the base.

The army, then, was not built of individuals. There was no *Army Strong* slogan to seduce young people into volunteering for military service. Nor was there an *Army-of-One* ideal to entice the individual with promises of a career to enhance personal ambitions while creating a vast, interlocking team of all of the services, winning glory in defense of America's national interests abroad. No, the first reality of military discipline was to disengage the mind and learn to follow orders automatically. Thinking—especially self-reflection—was not only discouraged, it was not allowed. All of our energy was directed toward achieving objectives that were larger than the individual lives we would be asked to lay on the line. From now on, we would have to live with the awareness of imminent death, and toward that end we would be relieved of our self-conscious expressions of individual appearance and behavior.

We were gathered at Fort Lee to complete the initial transformation from a civilian recruit to a soldier. Individuality was to be replaced with the *esprit de corps* of the unit. Our heads were shaved, and our civvies were replaced with ill-fitting, olive-drab fatigues and army boots for everyday wear, and an equally ill-fitting dress uniform for formal assemblies and to wear off base. Except for a few hours of off-duty time during the week, every activity of every day was prescribed, standardized and regimented.

John, Bob, Mike and I were assigned to the same basic training platoon headed by a drill sergeant. The entire platoon was lined up on the first floor of our barrack, and we stood at attention while the drill sergeant inspected us and selected the four recruits who would serve as squad leaders. Bob and I, along with two others, were chosen simply because, at twenty-one, we were two of the oldest recruits in the platoon and we both had almost three years of college education. Squad leaders were assigned to a room apart from the general barracks, and Bob and I roomed together on the second floor while the other squad leaders took the first floor.

We were each responsible for the men whose bunks lined one side of the dormitory, and we were equally culpable for infractions by members of our squad. So, it was my duty to see to it that each member of my squad maintained the cleanliness of his bunk-area and the prescribed orderliness of his gear. Once I had learned to meet those directives myself, I had to instruct the members of my squad and pre-inspect them so that the drill sergeant would not site us for infractions. Bunks were to be made smooth and tight enough for a quarter to bounce on the blanket, and each item of clothing had to be folded and stored in the footlockers at the end of the bunk, meeting standards of dimension and display. Boots were to be spit-shined.

Each day, orders were issued through the chain of command, from the battalion and company commanders to the drill sergeants to the squad leaders. They told us how we were to dress for training and when we were to align ourselves for inspections. There was a prescribed way in which we lined-up for those inspections, lined-up at the mess hall for meals and conducted ourselves when off duty.

Our duty was well defined. We had sworn an oath to defend the nation against all enemies foreign and domestic. Toward that end, we were issued a copy of the *Soldier's Handbook*, which began with a pledge of patriotism, "I am an American soldier...a protector of the greatest nation on earth..." and ended with a list of General Orders that ensured the uniformity and predictability of our actions.

Most of the men in our platoon, our company and our training battalion were in the WORWAC program, but we received no special treatment. The humiliation we endured at the hands of the instructors was intended to break down our sense of individuality and to secure our place under the command and authority of the military.

In spite of that, Bob, John, Mike and I remained close friends. Our initial meeting at the train station in Leesville had made the four of us feel bonded to each other, and so we were. Initiated by that circumstance, we supported and helped each other find our way in the strange, new environment of the army and, because of our close relationships to each other we did not lose our sense of individual relatedness or our humanity.

John was the most laid-back among us. He took the whole military experience in stride, because he was a twenty-year-old army brat, whose father was a retired army colonel. Nothing in our training surprised John, probably because his father had once commanded a basic-training camp. Thus, from an early age, John was accustomed to routine, order and discipline. He knew what to expect from the military, and he knew the ropes of basic training.

That familiarity with the military gave John an attitude. He had an air, not exactly of contempt, but of being able to see through the drama. When the sergeant shouted, "Attention!" the rest of us tightened our sphincters and stood erect, still intimidated by the authoritative voice-of-command personified by the perfect posture, physique and starched uniform of our drill sergeant. Like the rest of us, John followed the directive, but he sometimes had a little smirk that caused the sergeant to get right in his face and confront that attitude, to which John barked out "Yes sergeant" and "No sergeant" as required. But he was not intimidated. He stood a bit above the ground, playing along yet perfectly aware of the whole process of turning the recruit into a soldier. Because he understood the expectations so much better than the rest of us and carried himself with such confidence, John became a role model for me, strengthening my confidence in my ability to integrate into the military without losing my sense of self.

Bob was a Virginian of impeccable pedigree who claimed to be a descendant of the Confederate general Robert E. Lee, though mostly he kept his past and his family life a guarded secret. He was an integral part of our foursome, but he remained arrogant and apart with, it seemed, one foot always outside of the tight little circle of our comradery. Oddly detached from any display of sensitivity, he was always serious and not to be joked with.

Because of those deeply wounded sensitivities underlying his personality, I sensed that Bob and I were not so different. I could empathize with his attitude, but I was neither as hardened nor as angry as he was. If I teased him about a scuff mark on his spit-shined boots, or tried to touch his shoulder in a reassuring way, or probed too deeply in trying to discover who he was, he exploded in rage. We often got into arguments that, more than once, nearly came to blows. At such times, John would step in with his easygoing manner and sooth Bob's volatility. It seemed to me that Bob's attitude of detachment was unnatural and defensive. But I guess that defensiveness helped him keep his anger in check.

Mike was another army brat, but his father was still on active duty—a colonel assigned to the Pentagon. At nineteen, Mike was one of the youngest of the warrant officer candidates, and he carried himself with the youthful air of a soulful person. A quick glance, in which we caught each other's eyes, followed by shy smiles seemed to say that we were kindred spirits—guarded but, unlike Bob, not buried beneath an armor-shielded mask of indifference. The faint glimmer of Mike's soul beneath his ego-façade revealed that he too defied the process of self-alienation. But the look on Mike's face was also shaded with sadness that expressed a note of anxiety and uncertainty at having resigned himself to Fate—two emotions that also resonated with me.

The first time we were off duty and allowed privileges, Mike and I sat together drinking beer and sharing what little there was of two life histories that began with high school and culminated at a wooden picnic table on the patio of the Fort Polk PX. Mike was soft-spoken so that, at times, I had to strain to hear what he was saying. But I sensed that he adopted that soft-spoken posture to mask the deep intensity of his feelings. It lent him an air of mystery that I found intriguing, and it attracted me to him.

Mike spoke of his father with affection, but it was evident that the hardened, career military officer high up in the chain of command and bucking for his general's star was a stern man and a harsh taskmaster that provoked conflict with the sensitive nature of his only son. I told Mike about my family life, and I took mental notes as I compared the controlled pragmatism of my father with the stern discipline of the military officer.

Mike had attended a year of university but, feeling alienated from his peers and not inspired by his courses, he had dropped out—a tale of discomfort that was conspicuously familiar and cast the bonding hoops more securely around us. He had not found a job to set him on a career track, like I had found with Al Ramp, nor had he found a friend like I had found in Carl. It was then, it seemed, that Mike butted head-first against the paternalistic, militaristic structure represented by "the colonel," the name by which Mike referred to his father with a mixture of affection, respect and fear. As Mike related his story of dropping out of school and conflicting with his father, I could almost hear his father's words: *'Son, if you're not going to go to college, then you had better think about going into the military. No son of mine is going to turn into a goddamn hippy.'*

"Goddamn hippy," Mike repeated, digging his thumbnail into the soft wood of the tabletop. Then, he looked at me with a wiry grin. "Goddamn hippy!" we repeated together and laughed.

In spite of our different backgrounds, we all had a strong desire to fly—as though soaring on mechanical wings would somehow lift us up above the mundane reality of the world and set our spirits free. That was the common thread that bound all of the warrant officer candidates. Most of us, too, had college or university experiences with which we were dissatisfied.

Bob fell into those categories, though the information came out of him in bits and pieces, for all he ever said was that he joined the army to find excitement and adventure. I was beginning to suspect that he was running away to save himself from the boredom and frustration of a sheltered but angry and dissatisfying life. John joined the WORWAC program because it was his ticket into a profession in aviation.

In basic training, my squad and I shouldered our rifles in the cold rain of the Louisiana winter and, alongside the other squads in the platoon, sloshed twenty-miles through the mud to an overnight bivouac in the woods. Under the watchful eyes of the drill instructors, we spent days on the firing range, shooting at targets to qualify with our M-1 training rifles and to see who would become a designated "marksman." In combat simulation, we crawled on our bellies under barbwire, while sergeants shouted at us to keep our butts down because the machine-gun bullets whizzing just above our heads were live rounds. We ran obstacle courses in which we worked as a team to build our *esprit de corps*. Together, we endured the abuse of our instructors and drilled in formations until the whole platoon could move with the precision of one body.

We completed our training and stood at attention in structured rectangles on the parade field with other platoons of our company and other companies of our battalion. Flags waved. We turned smartly, marched in formation past the reviewing stand, received congratulations from the base commander and graduated. We had completed, together, the transformation from civilian recruit to soldier.

✵ ✵ ✵

As real soldiers, we now followed the events of the Vietnam War with greater interest. At home—a term that now seemed strangely detached from our life on military bases—anti-war demonstrations were mounted in San Francisco and New York. Those protests seemed far away, for the strict military routine shielded us from domestic opposition to the war effort of which we were now a part.

Richard Nixon, the Republican candidate for president, visited Saigon to show support for the government of Nguyen Cao Ky. He stated that anti-war protests in the United States were prolonging the conflict. General Westmoreland, the commander in Vietnam, agreed and publicly stated that we were winning the war. But privately he expressed concern to President Johnson that the war could go on indefinitely.

Either way, the command policy was for one-to-one replacement of troops on the battlefield on the basis of a one-year rotation. So, whether we were winning or expecting the war to continue, the training of replacements had to be intensified. As real soldiers, we were now engaged, and we did not want to miss our chance at the excitement and adventure of combat.

☆ ☆ ☆

We were sent directly from Fort Polk to Fort Wolters, Texas, where we received our primary training as helicopter pilots. The base was located in the arid country about thirty miles west of Fort Worth. Seen from the air, it looked like a grid superimposed on the undulating hills of the west Texas prairie. It had a well defined perimeter, neatly placed housing units with trim lawns, parade grounds, training classrooms and three airfields with row upon row of helicopters shining in the Texas sun.

After basic training, all WORWACs were promoted to the status of cadet and the pay grade of sergeants. Too, our lives were made a bit more comfortable. Instead of barracks, we were housed in buildings that had separate eight-man dormitories where we each had a bunk, a trunk, a wardrobe, a desk and a chair. Placement in the dormitories was by alphabetical order. Bob and John were each assigned to other dorms, but Mike and I were placed together. The bond between us grew. Eventually, my affection for Mike came to fill the emptiness I felt after my separation from Carl.

Carl and I had been exchanging letters. After he graduated from the university in January, he had been sent for eight weeks of advanced leadership training. About the same time that I was assigned to Fort Wolters, he was assigned to Fort Bliss near El Paso, Texas. He would pass through Fort Worth on his way to his command assignment. I was anxious to see him and knew I could get a weekend pass. I wrote, proposing that we spend a weekend together in Fort Worth. But his return letter was cold and blunt. He told me that it would be inappropriate for an army officer and an enlisted man to spend time fraternizing. *I hadn't expected that.* But Carl was now a career officer who took rigid military protocol—and perhaps himself—a bit too seriously. I had felt so close to Carl, and I was really hurt by that letter. On the other hand, I had found a new friend in Mike.

☆ ☆ ☆

It would be fifteen years before I would see Carl again. As fate would have it, his proficiency with the German language and his military specialty in artillery made him more valuable commanding a Nike Missile Installation in Germany, and he never did see combat in Vietnam. However, without combat experience, his opportunities for rising up through the ranks of the officer corps were limited. After eight years—when the Vietnam War ended—he left the army under distress and disillusionment and went into business.

☆ ☆ ☆

The program at Fort Wolters lasted for five months. It was intense and stressful with the constant threat that, by failing any phase of training, one could *washout* of the program and be recycled into the infantry. With that threat constantly hanging over our heads, it was even more important that the four of us remained supportive of each other. Mike and I developed a special friendship to share our triumphs and frustrations as we progressed through the training.

First, there was a month of academic courses composed of classes in aerodynamics, avionics, navigation, topography and meteorology.

The four of us passed all of the academic courses and felt euphoric as we anticipated our first day on the flight line.

At the airfield, hundreds of helicopters stood in neat rows, gleaming in the early morning sun, waiting for a student to strap himself into the seat, start the engine and engage the power to fly. There were two types of training helicopters. The Hughes TH-55 was specifically designed as an initial training helicopter though it was tiny and looked like a toy. We called it the *Mattel Messerschmitt*. I was assigned to fly the older Hiller OH-23 *Raven* that had been converted from an observation helicopter to a trainer. The cockpit had dual flight controls, for the student and the instructor. It had a central, pedestal-type instrument panel and a Plexiglas bubble that surrounded the cockpit so the pilots had clear vision all around.

My instructor pilot (IP) was a grizzly, middle-aged civilian contractor who had been training army pilots at Fort Wolters since the beginning of the program. He had a great deal of respect for us and for what we had volunteered to do, but he was also a no-nonsense kind of guy. His instructions were clear and he demanded obedience because he knew that the helicopter was a complicated and dangerous machine and that an inattentive student could kill him. He started his lesson by reiterating the aerodynamics that we had learned in the classroom and how these factors related to the flight controls.

To the left of the seat was the collective stick, hinged at the rear so that it could be lifted up or pushed down. "The *collective*," he explained, "controls the pitch on the rotor blades. Pull up to increase pitch—more bite on the air, more lift. That takes more power so there is a twist-grip throttle on the end of the collective stick—like a motorcycle throttle. You hold the collective by the throttle and when you pull up to increase pitch, you must simultaneously roll-open the throttle so that you maintain a constant rpm, which is noted here, on the tachometer."

He then explained the importance and operation of each of the various instruments on the control panel—tachometer, airspeed indicator, oil pressure gauge, fuel gauge, engine temperature gauge, outside air temperature gauge, altimeter, pitch indicator—and showed me how to set and operate the intercom and the radio.

"Once the engine is started," he continued, "the two spinning rotor blades act as a single rotor disc. The attitude of the rotor disc is controlled by the *cyclic stick."* The cyclic was between my knees. When the stick was tilted forward, it tilted the rotor disc forward and produced forward motion. Tilted sideways, it produced side movement and back-ward, back motion.

"When the rotor is spinning, it produces torque, or counter-spin. That small, side mounted rotor at the end of the tail boom is to counter the torque, and the pitch on the tail rotor is controlled by the left and right foot pedals." So, I had four limbs to handle five controls, all of which needed to be coordinated with precision to make the machine fly.

We strapped ourselves into the seat and started the engine. I watched the IP jockey the throttle while the twin rotor blades swung in a lumbering arc and picked up speed until they were spinning as a semi-solid disc above our heads. Then, his words crackling in my earphones over the loud whine of the engine, he pronounced his most important lesson. "You must always remember that you are the control unit of this machine. You do not strap yourself into the aircraft. You strap the aircraft onto your back." Then, effortlessly, he lifted the aircraft to a three-foot hover, turned into the wind and took off.

My first flight was just an orientation ride. Once we were at altitude and in straight and level flight, my IP let me take over the controls, just to get the feel of the aircraft in flight. Real instruction began with the second lesson.

The IP took me to an area about the size of a football field, marked off with white painted tires, and positioned the helicopter in the center of the field at a three-foot hover. Straight ahead of me, about 100 yards away, was a tree. One at a time, the IP turned the controls over to me with the instruction that I was to keep the aircraft three feet above the center of the field and pointed directly at the tree. First, he let me have the collective stick and throttle, until I was able to do a pretty good job of maintaining rpm while holding the aircraft not exactly at three feet above the ground, but close enough. Then, he let me take over the cyclic stick. All I had to do was to keep the aircraft positioned over the center of the field—or at least inside the four tires. My per-formance was good enough to let the IP know that I could feel the sensitive responses of the machine and had a good instinct for flying. Finally, he let me work the foot pedals to try to keep the aircraft pointed at that tree. I learned that hovering required the intense physical and metal dexterity to manipulate and coordinate all of the controls in precise harmony. Hovering is the most basic maneuver for helicopter flight, because it is the position from which all take offs are initiated and landings terminated.

Between lessons in hovering, my IP took me on flights during which he demonstrated the capabilities of the helicopter. We landed in tiny clearings in the woods, landed atop narrow mesas and descended in steep, tight spirals that had me holding on to the doorframe, my heart pounding with the thrill of riding an invisible rollercoaster in the air.

It took several more lessons and a concerted effort for me to learn to coordinate the five delicately balanced controls and maintain a static hover. As an adolescent, I had been clumsy so that learning to control the complicated machinery was a personal triumph over the physical and sensate functioning of my body. I coordinated the throttle, collective, cyclic and the two foot pedals so as to maintain the aircraft in perfect stasis amid the whirling vortex of the aerodynamic forces of wind and ground-effect currents. Then, my IP taught me how to take off and land.

The next important lesson was what to do if the engine quit. If a helicopter loses power, it can be safely landed in a maneuver called an *autorotation.* My IP explained that the autorotation was initiated by dropping the collective stick, so that the pitch on the rotor blades was decreased to a minimum. This caused the helicopter to descend in a controlled fall at a rate of about 2,000 feet per minute. The air flowing up through the rotor disc served to keep the blades turning, therefore maintaining rpm and providing enough lift to maintain control. At about fifty feet above the ground, I popped pitch on the rotor blades by pulling up sharply on the collective stick. The helicopter's controlled fall was arrested. At fifteen feet, I pulled in the rest of the pitch on the blades and set the aircraft gently and safely on the ground without damage or injury.

My first solo flight consisted of three circuits of the airfield and three touch-and-go landings. In order to keep from washing-out of the program, each cadet had to solo within the first fifteen hours of instruction. John, Bob, Mike and I all passed that milestone together. It was important to support and encourage each other, as though the failure of one would unravel the pact of our tightly knit foursome, and the rest would be forced to complete the training alone. When we had all sooled, we celebrated our triumph with a beer party at the PX, laughing about the mistakes we had almost made and expressing sincere admiration for the skill and patience of our instructors.

Though each IP paired two of his students together for shared hours and lessons in teamwork, learning to fly solo meant just that, and the majority of my time was spent alone with the aircraft, followed by rides with the IP to see if I had mastered the lesson of the day. The training area was huge. There were twenty-five staging fields that the army leased from the surrounding ranchers, and there were hundreds of landing sites scattered across the landscape.

During the next months, I spent over a hundred hours in the air. The butterflies in my stomach before each flight signaled the heightening of physical sensations as I learned to lift the aircraft smoothly to a three-foot hover, turn into the wind and glide forward into the take off. I learned to skim the ground at seventy knots, leap over tree lines and ridges and fly my body and my spirit into the astounding heights of the pale blue sky. As my sensitivities became attuned to the engine's surges of power, I could feel the bite of the rotor blades in the air. I was learning to fly *by the seat of my pants,* feeling the subtle changes in vibration that rose from the metal seat directly up my spine and entered my brain faster than the reaction time of eyes and ears. The physicality of flying seemed to by-pass the thought process, relying more on sensitivity and intuition. Thus, I learned the techniques that gradually released my mental faculties from attending to mechanical duties. As I began to master the technology, man and machine were merging at the unconscious level of instinct. It was then that I began to perceive my transcendent inner spirit being aroused within me.

When bound to the earth, our perceptive faculties equate objects to the human scale. The height of a building or a tree is unconsciously equated to the height of an individual; the width of a road or the distance across a lake is equated to an arm's length or the length of a stride; even the height of a distant mountain is measured in terms of feet, given meaning by its relationship to the scale of the human body. But then, when we rise to tens of thousands of feet above the earth in an airliner, the sheer immensity of the landscape is overwhelming.

Seen from that vantage, we lose sight of the earth's details and all that is left in our mind's eye is an abstract impression like those images captured, for example, in a Georgia O'Keefe painting. The land recedes into the background in muted shades of brown and green. The outline of distant mountains is rendered in shades of purple that vary with the depths of the shadows. The sky is blue. The clouds are puffs of gray and white, made milky and glowing at the edges by the light of the sun. Bound by human dimensions, the first view is physical. The other view, divorced from the human scale, is spiritual and an abstraction.

Unlike an airliner, a helicopter is nearly always flown relatively close to the ground, rarely raising more than a few thousand feet into the air. Thus, from a perspective somewhere between the human scale and an abstract impression, the senses are awakened to experience the landscape in a unique way that merges the physical and the spiritual. My proximity to the ground—usually only a few hundred feet of altitude—made all the difference in my perception, for I had to keep my attention intently focused on the contoured details of the landscape I was flying over. I saw those details close-up, from a bird's eye view, like that of a hawk in flight. From 500 feet, the darting eye of the hawk spies a rabbit dash out from its cover. He swoops down upon his meal. No languid impressionism there, for the bird is hungry.

Following the flight of the hawk, I swoop down to a sandbar in the river, touch my skids to the ground and take off again. I note the details of the water-carved riverbank, and the pink flowers on the cactus that clings tenaciously there. Deep, dry gullies and red sandstone mesas break the pattern of waving prairie grasses. On surrounding ridges and hills there are thickets of mesquite shrubs or a lonely oak tree outlined against the sky, and I feel like I can reach out and touch them. Flying that close to the ground at nearly a hundred miles an hour requires such highly tuned concentration that all my synapses are sparkling; my senses sharpened on the whetting stone of solitude.

I see the elements of the landscape as sculptures placed there by a skillful hand, the surgical scalpel of a titanic sculptor. I pull up on the collective and the helicopter rises to 1,000, 1,500, 2,000 feet. Now, rivers and streams appear as threads of light shimmering in the sun. Then, I swoop down close again so I can see the sun-dappled ripples in the stream, the pebbles on the shore and the horned lizard sunning itself on a rock. From 2,000 feet of altitude, the lines between barren earth and vegetation produce subtle and dramatic changes in texture and tone. But when I swoop down within a hundred feet of the ground, I can distinguish individual flowers in a field of bluebells, smell the sage colored grasses, taste the dry dusty plains covered with prairie dog mounds, where the vortex of my rotor spins dust devils and chases tumbleweed. Alone in the wilderness and keenly aware of the earth's details, I instinctively skim the ground and flow over obstacles in my path, like a sparrow heading home to nest.

With my flying machine strapped to my back, I feel the aliveness of the earth, and my spirit transcends the human dimension to experience the earth as a sublime architectural collaboration between God and Nature. I suddenly understand why humans symbolically equate the bird and the human spirit. The experience of flight re-awakens a deeply resounding spiritual part of my being that had been mysteriously ordained in an Illinois cornfield, a decade before.

I soar high and dive, again, toward the earth skimming the surface, flaring the helicopter to slow it, gently kissing the sandbar on the Brazos River with my skids and taking off again, feeling the power of the machine as I accelerate along the ground and swoop up into the sky. I pull the aircraft into a steep climb, circle a high bluff along the river's edge and land on a pinnacle of rock with a panoramic view out over the arid wilderness. I had to piss.

I locked down the controls of the aircraft, leaving the rotor turning with the engine at idle, and stepped out onto the top of the mesa. It was a tiny landing pad with steep walls that fell three hundred feet to the river below. Puffs of clouds floated above me. A fresh breeze blew over me from the southwest. The air, warm and clean, smelled of mesquite and cactus and the dust of the open prairie that stretched before me, punctuated with other mesa-topped pinnacles and split by the shimmering path of the Brazos River that wound its way out of the west and disappeared in the haze of the eastern horizon. Here, I was alone in the wilderness. I lost all sense of the human dimensions of my body and, for a moment, felt the immensity of my own spirit unlimited by definition. I closed my eyes and raised my arms, allowing that moment to wash over me, feeling at one with the earth and sky.

As I turned back to my helicopter, I noticed two vultures sitting together on a branch of a naked tree that grew out of a crevice on the side of the mesa. Their black wings were folded behind their backs and their pock-marked red heads bent forward, following my movements with their beady eyes. I threw back my head and greeted them with a laughter that mocked their expectations and masked the twinge of anxiety that surfaced from my unconscious repertoire of ominous symbols. The vultures flew away, but they left me with the feeling that my solitary actions did not go unnoticed by universal powers more omnipotent than the United States Army.

The army knew exactly what it was doing by arousing the spirit that accompanied the solo aviator on flights in the wilderness—the spirit that separated the *real* aviators from the *wannabes* who, over the five months of training, never quite got the feel for the aircraft. These poor guys washed out of the WORWAC program and were sent to infantry units in Vietnam. What we did not yet understand, however, was that our feel for the aircraft—the merger of our instincts with the machinery—was designed to leave our minds free for further indoctrination. After five months mastering the machines of war, we were ready to become warriors.

For the third and final phase of training, our class of about three hundred warrant officer cadets—officially designated *WORWAC Class 67-21*—was re-assigned to Fort Rucker, Alabama. We were given four day's travel time. Standing in formation with our cadet commanders and the training cadre, we were given our orders, issued by the base commander: *"At 5 pm on the forth day, you will be at the roll call at Fort Rucker; present or accounted for, mister, or you will be listed as A.W.O.L. Do you understand me?"*

"SIR, YES, SIR!"

✲ ✲ ✲

Toward the end of our training at Ft. Wolters, I had saved enough money to purchase a car, a red Pontiac convertible. Mike and I decided to drive to Alabama together and spend three nights along the way in

New Orleans—the sensual jewel of the South. Elated to be away from the ever-watchful eyes of the military for the first time in seven months, we arrived in New Orleans late in the evening. We found a motel that promised us a large room with two beds for the other two nights if we could make due with a single room for one night. Neither Mike nor I objected, though the sight of the single king-sized bed in which we would sleep together stirred something deep inside me that conflicted with the homophobia ingrained in our culture. We looked at each other for a moment then mentally shrugged off the implication.

My affection for Carl had been much different than my affection for Mike. Carl awakened my sense of adventure, but he did not touch the deep sensuality that I had kept hidden throughout my adolescence. Through the mysterious combination of fate, timing and similarities in our upbringing, Mike and I both awakened those buried sensitivities in each other, for he, too, had suffered in his adolescence, much as I had. The deep innate feelings that we had both kept suppressed, hidden behind our fathers' disciplined and pragmatic expectations of us, were now awakened through mutual recognition.

These physical feelings were stimulated as well by our flight training that relied so much on sensation and intuition. Through the sensuality and spirituality of the experience of flying, we were both driven toward a feeling-toned relationship with the machinery and, subsequently, toward a feeling-toned relationship with each other. Recognizing those qualities in each other was part of what made us special friends. I had no reason to believe that Mike's affection for me was any less sincere than mine for him. Though we never expressed it physically, that affection bound us soul-to-soul, and we made each other high just being together.

During the last month of our training, when we had weekend passes, the two of us had taken my car to Fort Worth or Dallas. Neither of us liked to go to bars. Instead, we went to movies, ate in nice restaurants and—responding more to the hetero-conditioning of our upbringing than to any real desire—went looking for girls, but never with enough enthusiasm to pick them up. I just liked being with Mike, and I felt as though he just liked being with me.

Back at the base when we were off duty, we usually spent our time with John and Bob. But even when the four of us were together,

I studied Mike's face, etching it into my memory. He had soft, doe-like brown eyes with long lashes—dreamy and muted. His nose and face were chiseled in proportion to the slenderness of his body, not bony but warm and kind. The softness of his words were almost whispered and had the deep and abiding rhythm of a poet not quite born out of an adolescent shell—an impression accentuated by his resemblance to a young Bob Dylan.

Sometimes we just walked together, not close enough to touch each other but close enough so that by reaching out with our feelings, in the same way that we reached out with our feelings to merge with the helicopter, we could feel the movement of each other's bodies beneath our loose-fitting fatigues. The powerful sensation of relating to each other in that way made us feel adolescent and giddy. In the evening when I helped him with a math calculation in one of our academic courses, I put my hand on his shoulder. He leaned into it with the bone of his shoulder blade pressing against my hand just enough to show me that he wasn't going to flinch at my touch.

With those physical signals, we reassured each other that our feelings were not just abstract reactions to the insensitivity of our situation in the military, but were real feelings, powerful, intimate and shared. In a system that encouraged individual isolation and detachment, we kept alive our relatedness to our own humanity, with all of its individual frailty and vulnerability. Still, we remained self-conscious that others might have seen our relationship as too close.

But intimacy among warriors did not need to be conditioned by sexual-phobia. In high school I had read *The Iliad*. In class, we discussed the love between Achilles and Patrocles, and there was speculation and some giggles over whether or not homosexuality was implied. As with most things from that ancient culture, the relationship between those warriors simply did not fit easily into our contemporary models of manhood. The Greeks knew *Eros* not only as a god of love, but also the powerful god that united all things. He was the god of friendship, honor and courage, as well. They named that special friendship between warriors, *philos*—a powerful passion-of-caring that goes beyond the esprit de corps of the unit and becomes a special bond between individuals who share the warriors' experience. Mike and I had not yet been in combat together, so we could not yet fully appreciate the power of the bond that formed during training. But we had each experienced the intensity of the spirit that arose with the power to fly. That spirit knew that it wanted to be bound to another. Mike and I both accepted the need for philos, with the certainty that neither one of us wanted to go through our warrior's initiation alone.

Though we had been together for seven months, we had always been with others. We were trapped in the military structure so that our intimacy was restrained by its confines. Now for the first time we were alone together in a motel room in New Orleans and sharing a bed.

The room was blackened by the opaqueness of the motel curtains. I awoke in the middle of the night. Turned away from Mike's side of the bed, I clutched the cover more tightly about my chin. The saltpeter that we all agreed the army had been feeding us to stifle our sexual urges had worn off and, for the first time in a long time, I had an erection. It strained against the elastic band of my underwear wanting to be touched, though I dared not touch or move it for fear that the movement would awaken Mike. I listened for the sound of his breathing, but there was nothing but silence.

Was he, too, lying awake staring into the darkness with the same unmentionable thought crossing his mind? The unmentionable thought was that I wanted to touch him. Reaching out with our feelings was one thing, but I wanted to touch him with my hands. I wanted to break through the existential isolation of the past seven months where, under the watchful eyes of the military, we did not even throw our arms around each other's shoulders as we strolled from the PX yet, in the communal bathroom of our billet, we showered naked together every day. Now I wanted to feel his hand in mine. I wanted to stroke the smoothness of his cheek, run my fingers through his hair, and with his face close to mine I wanted to taste his breath. I wanted to hold him, press our bodies together and kiss him.

What if he reciprocated? What if Mike, the soft poet with the sad eyes, wanted—needed—to touch me as much as I needed to touch him? Could we take a chance on exploring the depth of our passion-of-caring for each other—a passion that, if ever discovered, could ruin both our careers in the military? Could we trust each other? Slowly, I rolled onto my back so that I could glance at his side of the bed and let my fingers move slowly toward him.

Mike was gone. I panicked. For a moment, I thought that he might have somehow sensed my feelings for him and scurried out of the room in the middle of the night. But Mike was not timid. He wouldn't do that. Perhaps he'd had the same feelings toward me but, lying there awake in the dark with his own boner, cautiously stretching his hand toward my side of the bed, he had heard the voice of his father, "the colonel," echoing in his head. *'Don't go there, Mike!'* And he escaped into the cool of the night to allow his passion to wilt.

The tension of my mixed emotions was so powerful that I wanted to masturbate, but I didn't. Then, the door opened and Mike crept quietly back into the room. I rolled to my side of the bed and pretended to be asleep, but I listened intently while he took off his shoes and socks, pulled his shirt off over his head, unbuckled and unzipped his pants and laid them across the chair where he had put them earlier in the evening. Then he climbed quietly back into the bed, being careful not to disturb me, and rolled to his side, tugging lightly on the cover.

I listened to him for a long time, taking in everything, taking in as much of Mike—as much of my philos—as I dared in the darkness and the silence of that New Orleans motel room. I felt my pulse and the soft pounding of my heart reacting to his closeness, the muzzled desire and the death of a hope that dared not rear its head.

The next day we got our double room and both relaxed a little, though a lingering sense of sexual tension remained and we each caught each other doing alone what, the night before, we might have contemplated doing together. I was in the shower and, with the water running and a towel around my waist, I stepped into the room to grab the shampoo from my bag. I had left Mike sitting up in his bed, shirtless, reading, but when I surprised him he quickly adjusted the sheet to cover himself and hide the shame of taking his sexuality in his own hand. Catching him like that confirmed that we were *both* receptive to the subtle vibration of the sexual tension in the air and vindicated my feelings of the night before. I wanted him to know that, with me, there was no shame. "Sorry," I said with a smile, offering a word to shatter the web of guilty tension. Then I stayed in the shower long enough to give him time to finish alone what we could not bring ourselves to do together.

Later, he caught me the same way, when he had been out of the room and came back unexpectedly. "Sorry," he said with a sheepish grin and left again to wait for me in the motel coffee shop, where I later joined him for dinner.

Had it been only a question of sexual gratification, sensual New Orleans was an easy place to find a whore. Mike confessed that he had never been with a professional, and I was limited to one not very satisfying experience. It was not casual sex but intimacy that I desired. Those few days in New Orleans were a brief respite from the military—an opportunity to flirt with intimacy with another male that, in American society of the 1960s, was still an unmentionable desire. I could not know what thoughts were in Mike's mind but, disciplined as we both were by the expectations of our upbringing and our stature in the military, I don't know how far either of us could have gone in acting on that desire.

So the flirtation with an unthinkable act remained nothing more than that—never mentioned, never acknowledged. It was as though our two spirits—each encased in a transparent bubble—peered into each other's eyes and pushed outward on the membrane. We did touch hand-to-hand with only the finest film of separation between us, but still it was separation. We could not merge our spirits in a moment of intimacy to dispel the pain of detached, existential separation and feel that our lives were shared with love. The awkward knowledge of that predicament fell heavily on both of us with the awakened realization that the spirit encased in the transparent bubble was the embryo of the warrior, and the warrior was, indeed, the sole property of the warlords of the patriarchy.

By the summer of '67, the politicians and the warlords were feeling the pressure to deliver results in Vietnam. Anti-war sentiment was growing and tension over the war was dividing America.

The hawks in the administration, Johnson, McNamara, Bundy, swooped down on the doves and condemned the protests as unnecessarily prolonging the war. But the doves outflanked them by moving to the international arena. Organized by British philosopher Bertrand Russell, a mock war-crime tribunal was held in Stockholm, Sweden, which condemned U.S. actions in Vietnam and, by extension, the ambitions of imperialistic America that, to the rest of the world, were beginning to look much the same as soviet expansionism.

President Johnson publicly urged the North Vietnamese to accept a peace compromise, but Hô Chi Minh would not yield. Secretary of Defense McNamara testified before the Senate that the US bombing campaign, which had been going on for nearly three years, had failed to have an impact on the ability of the North Vietnamese to wage war. He stated that nothing short of virtual annihilation would succeed. Echoing McNamara's assessment, frustrated field commanders devised their own solution to winning the war that trickled down to us in our training camp.

"The only way to win the war," they said, "is to put all the good Vietnamese on ships; take the ships out to sea and nuke the whole country. Then, sink all the ships."

Kill them all. The only victory lay in genocide.

☆ ☆ ☆

Mike and I arrived at Fort Rucker in time to change into our uniforms and fall-in at that five o'clock formation, as ordered. We were assigned not to barracks or dormitories but to two-man suites, each with a sleeping room with two twin beds and a study room. We were allowed to choose our own roommates, and Mike and I agreed to room together while John and Bob also shared a suite. Mike and I accepted how firmly the military authority asserted itself over our spirits. The unthinkable, unfulfilled desire for intimacy that I had felt in New Orleans was suppressed. There would be no relapse.

Our training at Fort Rucker began with learning to fly on instruments. The helicopter that we used was known to civilians as a "whirly-bird" and, with its Plexiglas bubble and an open-frame tail boom, was a familiar sight in urban skies and on television. The army had employed it since the Korean War, where it was used primarily for medical evacuations. The beefed-up training model—the Bell TH-13—had a full array of instruments. We flew with an IP, but wore a hood that was fitted over our helmets so that it blocked outside vision and forced us to fly using only the indications of the instruments. The orientation to instrument flight was a practical and essential part of our training. Lost in a cloud, for example, a pilot's vertigo and disorientation put the helicopter and crew in danger that was much more extreme than in a fixed wing aircraft because of the possibility of rolling-over—a maneuver that spelled death. Thus, it was imperative that we learned to trust ourselves to the readings on the instruments. But the more nuanced lesson was the continued merger of man and machine. The warlords of the patriarchy were turning us into efficient control units of the machinery of war.

We then learned to fly the workhorse of the Vietnam War, the UH-1 (Huey) helicopter. After spending several weeks transitioning into the heavier and more complex aircraft, we began a long period of tactical training that made us proficient pilots by practicing tactical maneuvers over the humid forests of southern Alabama, along the Chattahoochee River on the border with Georgia and over the scrub-covered dunes of the Florida panhandle. Our mechanical proficiency with the aircraft was honed as a tactical instrument of war.

We learned to land in small staging areas in the forest to simulate troop insertions and extractions. We flew sling-loads, carrying supplies beneath the aircraft in a sling connected by a long cable. We flew gun-ships, strafing the firing-ranges with live ammunition. We flew night missions and tight formations, both in daylight and at night, with less than a rotor-diameter of distance between the tips of our rotor blades, as we would do in Vietnam. And we learned to fly low-level, following the contours of the earth and its vegetation at 100 miles an hour, as we navigated to distant staging areas or outlying airfields.

While our training as warriors was becoming more intense, our indoctrination to the enemy was overly simplistic. We were issued a thin pamphlet that briefly discussed the culture and people of Vietnam in simple terms and were instructed to read it in our spare time. We were told that we would need this orientation in the eventuality that our aircraft would crash or be shot-down in hostile territory. We were also taught escape-and-evasions techniques. But mostly we were indoctrinated into the reality of the warrior's confrontation with death.

Through a series of lectures and live-action combat documentary films, we were being psychologically manipulated—brainwashed—into how we *should* think about the war. The military professionals who trained us carefully orchestrated the discussions that followed each session, so that any questions about our government's policy in Vietnam were circumvented. Just as we were being trained as control-units for the machinery of war, we were being trained as instruments of that government policy, not as critics of it. Each of the lectures and training sessions ended with the same tone of finality that reiterated the military objectives of the war. *You're being trained as pilots but, first and foremost, you are soldiers. You are going to Vietnam to kill gooks.* That simple lesson summed up the military's objective: The soldier's creed was to destroy the enemy and his will to continue with the fight. Those lessons were intended to evoke and instill in us a killer instinct.

We were all affected in different ways by the subtle evocation of the killer instinct. In young, nonprofessional military recruits, encouraging the killer instinct was a dangerous challenge to our sanity. We followed through the course of our training with blind obedience, trying to keep our faith that the military establishment knew what it was doing and that the nation would not abandon us. Still, there were faults in the training—unanswered questions that left us uncertain of the limitations placed on the roles we would play in the combat zone.

Those questions concerned our relationship to the Vietnamese. We were fighting on behalf of the government of South Vietnam, but the pamphlet that the army had given us taught us very little about the Vietnamese people, hardly anything of their culture and nothing about the cultural differences between the north and the south—those subtle differences that made one the "bad guys" and the other our allies. Graphic and dramatic combat orientation films and lectures distorted the enemy into faceless, dehumanized gooks and overshadowed the simplistic lessons of the pamphlet. Combat atrocities were accentuated in a way that made the gooks—and by association all the Vietnamese people—seem less than human. Moral questions about killing gooks were neatly circumvented. Those lectures did not stimulate well-reasoned discussions of why it was acceptable to kill certain Vietnamese and not others. They were aimed at our feeling-toned responses, making us feel in our guts that killing was an integral part of the warrior's creed.

Furthermore, we were made to feel alone with that creed. Detachment, we were told, was the soldier's greatest emotional security. Close friendships between soldiers were discouraged because the death of a close comrade could devastate our effectiveness as soldiers. It had happened in WWII and in Korea, and it was already a proven fact among infantrymen in the field in Vietnam, where the death of a soldier's special friend, his philos, either threw him into a deep depression or enraged him into berserk fury. Both of those attitudes endangered the unit. The army tried to replace individual closeness with esprit de corps. It represented an ideal loyalty to the unit and went hand-in-hand with the policy of one-on-one replacements in the field. However, I felt that the lesson was particularly aimed at helicopter pilots. It encouraged us to wed ourselves to the machinery that we controlled so as not to become distracted by personal relationships that would limit our efficiency.

But that policy of the warlords completely disregarded fateful encounters and the chemistry between people. The intimate relatedness that Mike and I had so laboriously developed was directly assaulted by military policy and by subtle hints from our commanders and classmates that if we showed too much mutual affection we would be ostracized and cast out for offending the ingrained esprit de corps.

I could feel Mike's spirit being transformed. Our unspoken desire for physical intimacy had been buried, yet we retained our sensitivity to each other. Still, we dared not look into each other eyes and smile—not in public and, eventually, not even in the confines of our own rooms, where the door was always open. We no longer touched each other. I could feel the warmth of his character leaching away as his sensitivities, like my own, were being fine-tuned to those of the modern warrior. Thus, our feelings for each other changed.

As the killer instinct merged with the spirit of the warrior-aviator, I sensed that Mike's inherent alertness and clarity of thought were being transformed by the ever-present knowledge that we all faced the real possibility of death. He remained soft-spoken, for that was a solid, ingrained attribute of his personality. But a punctuated staccato replaced the smooth and gentle poetry of his speech. His feelings turned cold and sometimes stabbed my feeling for him, inflicting an icy wound. The same conditions that turned Mike's warm sensitivities into frigid alertness, finely tuned to the defensive posture of self-survival, also turned my romantic passion for the adventure of war into the glory-seeking grandiosity of an inflated warrior spirit.

I could not remember a single defining moment when that wonderful inner spirit that I had first sensed in the moonlight of an Illinois cornfield was reawakened, and I became a warrior who soared into the solar heights on mechanical wings. It was only in subtle ways that my surrender to Fate was commandeered by the warlords of the patriarchy, who offered up my spirit to the god of war. Perhaps my transformation was invoked by indoctrination films and lectures, perhaps by the secondhand war stories that we repeated to ourselves while drinking beer in the PX. Perhaps it was the constant threat of death hanging over me, or my simple acknowledgment that we were all going to combat assignments in Vietnam and that the time was drawing close when some of us would die. Perhaps my surrender was invoked by the esprit de corps and by indoctrination to a responsibility that put service to the nation above individual lives. Perhaps all of those things tapped into my hidden inner rage, into the fire deep down inside that rose up in anger to defend myself.

More important, but also more exciting and more frightening, I was beginning to see things in my own nature that I had never acknowledged before. During my adolescence, the warrior spirit had remained silent, eclipsed by the sorrow I felt after my mother's death and the domesticated expectations of my father and society. But there was anger and frustration deep down in the crucible of my soul that sometimes leapt to life when I fought with my brother, Bill, and could easily be molded to serve the purposes of the god of war. The military did not need to instill the warrior spirit in me. It was already there, just waiting to be born, and now it had been handed a license to kill.

With that warrior spirit came blood lust: the violence out of which the warrior is born into the fullness of his manhood. I began to anticipate my first kill, my first taste of blood. Boiling up out of immeasurable time, the creed of the warrior demanded the taking of life. At that moment,

I would mysteriously inherit that life and would be fully recognized as a warrior and a man. The adventure of this war stirred my blood with passion, wedded me to the killer instinct to assure my success in the confrontation with death and made the taste of blood a precondition for the fulfillment of my initiation.

☆ ☆ ☆

Now, toward the end of our training, my warrior spirit—though standing still in the shadows just behind my veil of consciousness—became a companion to the instincts I had been trained to follow. Our final exercise was in military strategy. Each cadet was required to write a strategic plan that engaged almost 400 flight school cadets and officers and over 200 helicopters and encompassed our entire training area as a field of operation. One plan would be chosen by the tactics instructors and executed by the entire class.

Most of the cadets had a rather blasé attitude about the exercise, knowing that it would not effect their graduation or commissioning. But the exercise stirred me into action, and I let my instincts take over. I studied the topography of the tactical operations area and located the installations and staging areas that were important for a realistic strategic assault. Then, I wrote the details of my plan with passionate clarity. When the tactics instructors chose my plan, I was assigned to be the commander of the class exercise on the final day of training.

That day, I did not fly a helicopter. Instead, I established my command post high above the action in a lumbering U-6, a fixed-wing aircraft piloted by one of the tactics instructors. Airborne just before dawn, we began flying circles at an altitude of 5,000 feet above Fort Rucker. By the time my classmates reached their helicopters, the yellow-orange fireball of the sun had risen on the eastern horizon and burned away a light veil of ground fog. The crisp, cool air of December promised perfect weather for the military operation I had planned—an airmobile assault that followed the example established by the army's airmobile divisions that were operating in Vietnam.

I watched from my command post as, on my orders, the pilots ignited the turbine engines of their transport helicopters and gunships, forcing each pair of twin blades to turn in a lumbering arc, rapidly pick up speed and merge into a semisolid disc above the aircraft fuselage. Again on my orders, the helicopters, located a three different airfields, rose in delta formations of fives and sevens. They climbed to their assigned altitudes and turned toward their military objectives. I had issued operational orders to each of my unit commanders, and now my job was to monitor the exercise. The pilot of my airborne command post climbed in a graceful spiral to 10,000 feet and turned southwest toward the center of the operational area so that we could keep visual and radio contact with all of the various tactical units.

The gunships flew in waves over the firing ranges, strafing the ground with live machine gun fire, their accuracy confirmed by the red streaks left by tracer rounds. Transport ships then landed in staging areas to simulate the disgorging of troops. Other aircraft simulated medical evacuations and logistic support of ground units, as well as exercises for refueling.

When all the military objectives had been met, I ordered my units to assemble in a single, grand formation at a point twenty miles south-southeast of the base. Then over 200 helicopters, in delta formations of five aircraft, descended to an altitude of 700 feet and flew over the base. The "whop, whop" sound of the rotor blades shattered the air, and the miles of tightly formed rotor discs cast a shadow over the ground in salute to the personnel who had trained us. I followed them over the base then gave the final order to break formation and "head for home." My classmates landed and threw their hats in the air—a gesture that symbolized the completion of nearly eleven months of hard training.

My pilot and I had to land alone at the fixed-wing airbase. None of my classmates were there, and I stood alone on the tarmac, smiling victoriously to myself. Whatever purposes there were to war, I thought, unfailing glory for the individual and the nation ranked at the top of those purposes. I basked in my moment of triumph, and I was confident—though this had only been a training exercise—that I had within me the capacity to shine in battle and to see my glory-star fixed forever in the firmament.

My pride was quickly dampened by the attitude of my classmates and tempered by the gentler chiding of my friends. Only when the fire of my victory-dance had been reduced to a smoldering ember was I welcomed back into the fold and esprit de corps of the class that had won both commission and wings.

Our graduation was a formal ceremony that all of our families attended. Dressed in our new, smartly tailored, dress-blue uniforms, we were issued our warrants, our bars and our wings. John, Bob, Mike and I celebrated together through the night. We were all granted leave to spend the Christmas holidays with our families, and ordered to report to various bases on the West Coast for transport to our units in Vietnam.

John was going to continue training, learning to fly the new *Cobra* gunships at Fort Stewart, Georgia, and he planned to marry his long-time sweetheart, Christine. But Bob, Mike and I would not attend the wedding. We were ordered to report to Fort Lewis, Washington and would still be together for the flight to Vietnam.

I spent Christmas with my family in Oak Park. It was a tense time of joy and anxiety, sharing what everyone knew might be our last Christmas together. In January of 1968, I flew to Seattle and, with two of my closest friends from a year of training, on to Vietnam via Alaska and Japan.

CHAPTER FOUR:

Vietnam

Au Co was the youngest and most beautiful princess in the 36th heaven. When the fiery heat of the golden-red crow had departed from the sky and the wild ivory-white swan bathed the night with its soft light, Au Co pulled back the veil of clouds and gazed down upon the newly formed earth. She and her sisters giggled as they transformed themselves into beautiful white Lac birds and flew down from the 36th heaven to light upon the ground. There, on a hillside by the pink mountains they transformed back into princesses and laughed and sang as they danced on the slopes. After a while, Au Co broke away from her sisters and, taken by the fragrance of the pink earth, she scooped some in her hand, lifted it to her mouth and tasted it with her tongue. "Don't do that!" shouted her older sisters. But it was too late. When the sisters transformed themselves back into Lac birds and flew back to the 36th heaven, Au Co found that the taste of earth had made her too heavy and that she could no longer return to her home. Frightened and alone, she leaned against the boulders of the pink mountains and wept for a thousand years.

Her tears formed a wide, sweet river that flowed down to the sea. Lac Long Quan, the Dragon Prince and son of the Sea Dragon tasted the new current of water that flowed down from the land, perfumed with the fragrance of the pink earth. He jumped onto the shore, transformed himself into a beautiful young man and followed the river inland, determined to find the source of the sweet water. When he discovered the princess Au Co, weeping alone high up in the mountains, he was spellbound by her beauty. She stopped crying, looked into the eyes of the noble young prince and told him her story, from the moment she had pulled back the veil of clouds until she realized that she could no longer return to the 36th heaven. The Dragon Prince sat down with her and told her of the loneliness of his own life beneath the sea.

Both marveled at the beauty of the earth, the freshness of the grasses and the fragrance of the flowers, but they soon realized that without Au Co's tears the rivers dried up and the land grew parched. Then Lac Long Quan had an idea. He took a vial of Au Co's tears down into the sea, down into the cloud chamber with its high jade pillars draped in fog deep in the palace of his father, the Sea Dragon. He mumbled a mantra and the ceiling of the chamber parted, ushering forth puffy white clouds from the sea. The first rainfall was the source of life for trees and grasses, birds and flowers and all living things upon the earth.

The love between Lac Long Quan and Au Co grew strong. Soon after they were living together on the earth, Au Co laid a sac of one hundred eggs. From the union of the Goddess and Dragon sprang a progeny of one hundred children. They grew as quickly as flowers in the field. Their parents gave them language to name all the things on the earth and taught them to make tools and to build houses and to net fish and to hunt game in the forest and to grow rice. Though the children of the earth were half-goddess and half-dragon, as humans they were mortal. Each generation passed the land on to the next. Under the guidance of the Goddess and the Dragon, the people grew strong.

Then one day, Lac Long Quan was standing by the shore and felt a curious twitch in his arm. He knew that he was being summoned back to the sea palace to take his father's place upon the throne of the Dragon King. He promised to come back to the land as soon as the coronation ceremony was finished, but Au Co knew in her heart that she would not see him for a long, long time. Alone, the Goddess retreated to the high mountains to await the return of her beloved Dragon.

(After Thich Nhat Hanh, "The Dragon Prince" and "One Hundred Eggs." *The Dragon Prince*, Parallax Press, Berkeley, 2007.)

In the year 2879 BCE, the children of the Goddess and the Dragon created a nation and called it *Xich Quy,* which was ruled from the royal city of *Tonquin* and made up of the eighteen kingdoms of the *Hong Bang* Dynasty. Fifteen hundred years before the Greeks brought their form of civilization to Western Europe, the Vietnamese had organized the most stable, prosperous and civilized nation in Asia, with its own administrative, social and economic institutions.

Xich Quy was conquered by the Chinese in 110 BCE and made a province of China. The big dragon ruled the little dragon for the next 1,000 years. Then, *Dinh Bo Linh* organized an army and drove the Chinese out. For another 800 years the Vietnamese forced back attempts at re-conquest by the Chinese and an invasion by the Mongol hoards of Kublai Khan. They absorbed the Champa Kingdom of the central coast and the part of the Khmer Empire that spilled over into the Mekong delta from Cambodia. But the people of Vietnam's many kingdoms fought among themselves. Then in 1802, Emperor *Gai Long* united Vietnam and established his imperial capital in the city of Hué.

The French came in the 1840s, conquered Vietnam, Laos and Cambodia and called the region Indochina because it sat at the cross-roads of Southeast Asia and each of its distinctive cultures exhibited elements from the cultures of both India and China.

At the Versailles Conference that ended World War I (1919), a young, 29-year-old anti-colonial political agitator by the name of Hô Chi Minh asked President Woodrow Wilson of the United States to support an independent Vietnam. But American political involvement with the French was complex, and Wilson refused the request.

During World War II, the Vichy government in Paris cooperated with the Japanese to bring Vietnam under the de facto rule of Japan. Hô Chi Minh formed the *Viet Minh,* the "League for the Independence of Vietnam," and was given training and weapons by the OSS to fight against the Japanese. At the end of WW II, citing the American Declaration of Independence, Hô Chi Minh declared Vietnam independent.

But the American-European allies had a different view of world politics. At the Potsdam Conference (1945), the allied powers decided that the Nationalist Chinese would accept the Japanese surrender in Vietnam north of the 16th Parallel and the British would accept Japanese surrender to the south. The British quickly returned control of their sector of Vietnam back to the French. In order to keep any part of Vietnam from having to submit to Chinese rule, Hô Chi Minh negotiated for the temporary return of the French to the northern sector for five years. Then a united Vietnam was to be recognized as an independent state within the French Union. In 1949, when the French made it clear that they would not relinquish control, as agreed, Hô Chi Minh, with his military commander Vo Nguyen Giap, retreated to the mountains, the realm of the legendary Goddess, Au Co, to begin the insurgency that became known as the *First* Indochina War.

The US position remained ambivalent. President Truman urged the French to de-colonize. The French declared that they would not leave Vietnam until the rebellion was put down and the country unified. In support of that position, President Eisenhower created MAAG (the Military Assistance and Advisory Group) to aid the French, and US taxpayers shouldered most of the cost of the First Indochina War. After the French were defeated at *Dien Bien Phu* in 1954, Vietnam was officially divided at the *Ben Hai River,* the 17th parallel, creating— along with the divided nations of Germany and Korea—a third staging area for the confrontation between the Communist Block and the West.

In 1959, the Communist Central Committee of North Vietnam authorized the armed struggle for the reunification of Vietnam. The guerrilla campaign launched in South Vietnam, known as the *Second* Indochina War, was more of a popular insurgency, with the intent of overthrowing the authoritarian government of President *Ngo Dinh Diem*, reuniting the country and installing an honest government.

Though President Kennedy considered the South Vietnamese government corrupt and out of control in its repression of its own people, his administration supported Diem.   But when Diem's government began to falter in 1963, the US perpetrated a coup that brought about political instability and resulted in Diem's assassination. Hanoi seized the opportunity to increase support for the insurgency in the south. Three weeks after Diem was murdered, Kennedy was assassinated and Lyndon Johnson was sworn in as the 36th president of the United States.

In August of 1964, following the Gulf of Tonkin Resolution that gave President Johnson the power to wage war in Southeast Asia, the National Security Agency recommended the bombing of North Vietnam. On the ground, 100,000 Viet Cong insurgents were fighting against the Army of the Republic of Vietnam (ARVN) forces, backed by 12,000 advisors from MAAG. By early 1965, the number of US advisors had jumped to over 20,000.

When President Johnson authorized escalation of the ground war and direct involvement of US troops in April of 1965, the supreme commander in Vietnam, General Westmoreland, proposed a three-phase strategy to win the war: 1) commit enough troops to stop ARVN forces from losing, 2) drive the guerrillas out of populated areas, 3) launch a mopping-up operation in the countryside.

In the fall of 1967, with 500,000 US troops in Vietnam, Westmoreland and US Ambassador Ellsworth Bunker presented an optimistic report to the president, stating that the end of the war was in sight. In an interview with *Time* Magazine, the general taunted the VC. "I hope they try something because we are looking for a fight."

In January of 1968, Bob, Mike and I arrived at the Air Force Base at Cam Rahn Bay. We had all heard the news and knew of Westmoreland's optimism. If he were right, my one-year tour in Vietnam would be a breeze—a mopping-up operation to finish the war.

✫ ✫ ✫

My first impression of Vietnam was not that we were in a war zone, but of the beauty of the landscape. The Air Force Base and Naval port at Cam Rahn Bay were major facilities for receiving recruits and supplies. They were located beside a clear blue lagoon surrounded by lush green hills that rose to rugged peaks with sharp outcroppings of pink granite that wore the velvety green skirts of a tropical jungle. Beyond the base perimeter, there was a small village of thatch-roofed huts. A narrow valley, carpeted with rice paddies, lay to the north. At Cam Rahn Bay we were guided through the bureaucracy of paperwork so that we could move on to our combat assignments.

Bob, Mike and I were all assigned to the 1st Cavalry Division, a 16,000 man airmobile force composed of three combat brigades and three helicopter battalions, with a total of 434 helicopters. The 1st Cavalry Division had been sent to Vietnam by ship transport in 1965 and was based 36 miles inland along Highway 19 near the small town of *An Khe,* about 150 miles north of Cam Rahn Bay.

By 1968, the An Khe valley had been pacified and the combat units of the 1st Cav had recently departed for the north. Camp Radcliff, the military base at An Khe, had been turned over to the 4th Infantry and served as an in-country administrative and training facility. There, we would receive a weeklong orientation to the country and to the war before being sent to our operational units north of the old imperial capital of Hué.

Camp Radcliff was a civilized outpost that seemed far from the reality of the war. The large 20-man officers' tents were erected on wooden platforms and stood in neat rows with manicured lawns outlined by white-painted rocks. There were "friendly" Vietnamese who came onto the base during the day to do the maintenance and gardening work. Bob, Mike and I, along with other new arrivals, were assigned to the same tent.

It was important to me to have come this far in my military career with these two friends. Bob and I continued to tolerate each other with accustomed familiarity, but Mike remained the philos with whom I had shared the transformation into a warrior and with whom I hoped to share my blood-right initiation into manhood. Our training had transformed both of us, but we still cared for each other and we were still together in this perilous adventure. The intensity of our affection was changed but not diminished, and we had the right to anticipate that we would share the intense emotions of our battlefield initiation. We spent our days in An Khe holding on to that expectation.

During breaks in our training we were allowed day passes into town. An army truck with wooden side benches under a canvas cover rolled and bumped along dusty roads filled with bicycles and the brash roar of motorbikes to deposit our group in the center of town. An Khe was not very remarkable. Highway 19, the main street, was packed with pedestrians, bicycles, motorbikes, a few small cars and military vehicles that honked and pushed their way through the crowd. The paved road was lined with one-story stucco and concrete administrative and commercial buildings, but all of the side streets were dirt. The core of the town was surrounded by small houses some with well-tended gardens. Most of the houses had thatch roofs and were constructed of bamboo or woven rattan mats.

After almost a week in Vietnam, entirely restricted to military bases, this was my first opportunity to really see the country and to interact with the people. Mike and I spent the afternoon walking through the hustle and bustle of an open street market hunting for souvenirs, like tourists. In the late afternoon, we found a quiet restaurant on a side street near the market, where we sat by a window that looked out onto a street of packed red clay. We ordered noodle dishes with fish and an unforgettably pungent fish sauce called *nuoc mam*. Then we turned to each other, talked quietly, dropped our defenses just a little and tried, once more, to reach our hands through the bubble membrane that encased each of our warrior spirits, as if to finally acknowledge our arrival in the war zone and to try to reassure each other about a future filled with uncertainty.

Wisps of dust, turned pink by the filtered light of the late afternoon sun, danced on a warm, gentle breeze. Across the narrow street, a young girl stood in a doorway. She appeared to be Eurasian—perhaps, I thought, the bastard daughter of a French soldier and a Vietnamese woman. She was about twelve years old, with a glowing light brown skin, deep black eyes and long black hair. Her remarkable beauty set her apart from the bent peasants and common country folk that scurried by in black pajamas and conical straw hats. I couldn't take my eyes off of her. She wore a pretty, rose pink party dress that came down to her bare feet, not the typical *ao-dai,* the tunic dress worn by older girls and women. Swaying gently, almost like a flower in the breeze, she seemed to be singing to herself in a voice I could not hear.

She may have sensed that I was staring at her, for she looked up and our eyes met. While Mike and I ate our meal, she continued to stare at us, not in a beggarly way, but rather with a gaze of magical penetration, like a child who was not judgmental but filled with wonder and curiosity. It was my first contact: the first time I locked eyes with a Vietnamese and the first time, too, that my presence in the country was acknowledged by a descendant of the Goddess and the Dragon Prince. Not a warrior, not even an adult, she was a pretty young child who possessed the beauty and serenity of the princess from the 36th heaven. It made me want to turn inward to see what it was that she was looking at—what the Vietnamese, through that child, saw in me. Wasn't I just another invading soldier from across the sea?

She was still standing in the doorway when we left the restaurant to return to the base at dusk. The town was off limits after dark. Security was the issue. Trust of "friendly" Vietnamese was limited to the daylight hours, for even though the valley had been "pacified," we all knew the Viet Cong were there, mingled with the general populace, lurking in the shadows and waiting for the night.

Our weeklong orientation to our combat assignments was through lectures, charts and a guided tour along a simulated jungle pathway that introduced us to various types of improvised explosive devises, booby traps, trip-wires and pits filled with sharpened bamboo called *punji* stakes. These were the types of insurgency weapons confronted by ground forces, which we might encounter if we were shot down.

During the lectures, we were shown maps of the four US military zones that divided South Vietnam and were designated by Roman numerals: I, II, III and IV Corps. The combat units of the 1st Cav were operating in I Corps, about two hundred miles to the north. Under the command of Major General John Tolson, the division had the responsibility of pacifying an operational area, code named "Jeb Stuart," that stretched from the old imperial capital of Hué to the demilitarized zone north of *Quang Tri* province, and from the slopes of the Annamese Mountains to the coast of the South China Sea.

Though we were still far from the battlefield, in those few days of combat orientation, all my senses were finely pitched to the tuning fork of the warrior spirit, and I knew that in order to triumph over death I would have to further orient myself to the enemy's land, habits and personality. I grew impatient to reach the combat zone.

☆ ☆ ☆

The three of us were all assigned to the 1st Cavalry Division, but each to a different unit. Bob was going to a gunship platoon. Mike would be flying "slicks," helicopters used for troop transport. I was assigned to fly command and control missions for the headquarters company of the 3rd Infantry Brigade—a logical result of my successful strategic field exercise in flight school. We each had to take responsibility for our own transportation to the combat zone and said our goodbyes on the tarmac of the airfield at An Khe. I made a pledge to see Mike again at our new base camp, then I hitched a ride north on an Air Force C-130 Transport with another new warrant officer from my flight class who was assigned to the same unit.

Unlike my friends from flight school, "Wild" Bill Pickren was a professional soldier and thus different from the green recruits sent for a one-year replacement rotation to the war in Vietnam. He had already served one tour as a helicopter crew chief and now, having completed flight school, was returning as the new maintenance officer of the unit to which we were both assigned. I set aside my wounded sentiments over the separation from my friends and tried to be friendly with Bill, but he was deeply engrossed in his own thoughts. So I let the drone of the aircraft's engines hypnotize me, as I gazed out of the window, watching a landscape molded by the gods unfold in the warm tropical sun. We flew at an altitude of about 10,000 feet, so the details of the landscape remained sharp and did not fade into abstract impressions.

As I watched the sacred architecture of the land that stretched below me, my heart pounded with excitement at this first view of the enemy's territory. I wanted to concentrate on keeping my perceptions attuned to the spiritual dimension of the land in which the promise of my warrior spirit would finally be fulfilled. The sensation was still new, but each sublime evocation of that warrior within me was becoming more intense, bringing me closer to the deeper, more primitive instincts that contrasted sharply with the mechanized modern soldier that was the logical outcome of my training. Like my primitive warrior ancestors, I reached out to grasp a fleeting unity with the land in which I would confront death.

To my right were the blue waters and sandy beaches of the South China Sea. A ripple of sand dunes marched inland and merged with earthier soils as they approached Highway One, the road that paralleled the coast about ten miles from the shore. The hollows between the dunes were filled with the lush green of rice paddy grasses that changed hue and tone as the wind from the sea blew over them. Tiny fishing villages, consisting of only a few thatch-roofed huts, resided in narrow, protected inlets where narrow, black out-rigger fishing boats were drawn-up on the white sandy shore. Other thatch-roofed structures were visible throughout the roadless landscape, where footpaths and narrow trails, following the crests of dunes and the banks of streams, converged with the geometric lines of rice paddy dikes built by farmers.

Inland from the highway, the topography changed. The low, rounded hills marched persistently upward toward a rugged and majestic ridge of mountains. When the hills became steep, they were sculpted into level-terraced rice paddies that made a quilt-work of the landscape, contrasting sharply with the bands of dark green foliage that threaded around and between the paddies. These bands were composed of tropical fruit trees—orange, banana, mango, durian, papaya and sway-ing coconut and areca palms. Those leafy woods flowed with the shape of the land or followed geometric patterns, depending upon the whims of nature or the caprice of man. On the crests of hills, wilder vegetation grew that concealed mongoose, monkeys, pythons and an occasional tiger that wandered down out of the mountains.

Streams and canals cut through the land, carrying water to the fields and back into the wide lazy serpentine of rivers that flowed down out of the mountains. They glistened in the sun and formed wide, shiny paths that dispersed into a myriad of delta streams, before releasing their flow of brown silt to mingle with the blue waters of the sea.

The ridge of mountains from which the rivers flowed was covered with green foliage that swept sharply upward from the low hills to where it met the jagged stone cliffs that defined the summits of pinnacles and marched from south to north as a wall that set the Annamese Highlands apart from Vietnam's coastal plain. Behind those ridges, other mountain ranges and deep valleys faded into a gray-green haze where, I imag-ined, rainbow colored birds called to each other above the thick jungle foliage, and columns of North Vietnamese soldiers threaded their way south along twisting footpaths a hundred, two-hundred feet below the immense forest canopy.

Above it all, the sky was a crisp blue, dotted with the white puffs of clouds lit by a golden sun. The light streamed down on the land, creating a dynamic tableau of floating cloud-shadows. The whole land-scape vibrated with the interplay of tone and color that gave the land power, vitality and beauty. Those terraced mountains, hills and dunes were so invitingly habitable, tame and yielding that they might well have bordered on paradise, had it not been a war zone. A war zone evidenced by the blasted pockmark craters from B-52 bombing raids and the thick curls of black smoke left with *deadly* accuracy in the wake of low flying fighter-bombers dropping napalm on bamboo villages.

Our transport landed at Phu Bai, the airbase several miles south of the city of Hué. A helicopter from our unit had been sent to transport us to the 1st Cav's base called Camp Evans. We flew across the Perfume River that divided the modern city, built by the French, from the old imperial capital; flew passed the inner, royal sanctuary, the *Citadel*, with its magnificent array of palaces; and north along Highway One. We arrived at the 3rd Brigade's headquarters and landed on a dusty helipad atop a flattened hillock.

My first impression of Camp Evans abruptly deflated my view of the theater in which the war was being fought. It was an eye-sore that sat to the west of Highway One and north of the *Song Bo* (the Bo River), about fifteen miles north of Hué. The huge camp, perhaps a mile square, was dotted with denuded hills whose crests had been scrapped flat and marked with white lime to serve as helicopter landing pads. Filling the hollows between the hills was a city of olive-drab colored tents, dusty jeep trails and haphazardly strung bundles of electrical and communication wire. Mounds of machinery and logistical supplies lay unsorted, trucked in from Da Nang or from supply ships anchored off the coast or dropped into the camp, seemingly at random, by huge, CH-54 Skycranes—cargo helicopters that looked like praying mantises. Sandbag embankments to protect electrical generating equipment and sandbag bunkers to protect the men had been hastily constructed. Inflatable, black rubber fuel bladders, each in its own embankment, were strewn across an area the size of a football field. Motor pools and aircraft maintenance facilities stained the ground around them with dark patches of grease and oil. Gun emplacements of 105mm Howitzers were spaced at intervals—like sandbag turrets on a castle wall—that dotted the barbed wire perimeter. Mountains of "C" ration cartons were stacked behind canvas roofed mess halls. And everywhere the air was filled with grime and the repulsive smell of shit being burned in severed oil drums behind tall, olive drab latrines that stood out conspicuously against the dusty landscape.

Bill and I were greeted by Major Frix, the commanding officer of the Headquarters Company of the famous "Garry Owen" brigade. (It was called that because the 3rd Infantry Brigade was shaped from other military units that included the old 7th Cavalry—the famous "Garry Owen" regiment that had been commanded by General George Custer at the Battle of Little Big Horn.) Colonel Hubert Campbell, a full "bird" colonel—called that because his rank-insignia was an eagle—commanded the brigade, which was composed of three combat battalions, each commanded by lieutenant colonels.

The size of the brigade, nearly 4,000 men, required a full company, between 100 and 200 soldiers, just to perform administrative duties—from seeing to it that the soldiers got paid, to field medical and communication services, to delivering the mail. A helicopter platoon was assigned to the brigade headquarters company to perform command and control functions for all of the infantry units and to fly scout missions.

We had five Hueys outfitted with tactical operations command posts (TOCs), from which battalion commanders could direct and monitor ground operations, just as I had commanded my units from an airborne command platform in the strategic training exercise. But the TOC could be removed and the same aircraft used to deliver mail, carry individual soldiers to and from the base when necessary, transport non-combat supplies, deliver body bags and so on—all of which came under the general heading of "ash and trash" missions. In addition, we had three OH-13S Sioux helicopters—like the ones we had used for instrument training at Fort Rucker—that were assigned as scout aircraft—our most combat intensive mission.

Following the normal rotation routine for new replacements, I would begin by flying co-pilot in the Hueys for four months, and then transition to scouts for four months. I would end my tour as a command and control aircraft commander.

Because of his long experience with aircraft maintenance, Bill took on the duties of the unit's maintenance officer with accustomed familiarity. We were assigned to cots in a huge 20-man tent with the other pilots where we stowed our gear. After that, we were left on our own to get to know the men, integrate into the esprit de corps of the unit and further familiarize ourselves with the unit's mission. I introduced myself to some of the other pilots—Paul, Dale, Al, Doug, Steve and Phil—without knowing whether to embrace them as a band-of-brothers or look upon them as professional colleagues. In the end, I decided to reserve my friendship until I could get to know them better.

Wild Bill remained the one person in the unit with whom I felt some degree of comradery, simply because we had shared the experience of flight school. Although we had not known each other personally, our shared experience was enough to give me some sense of orientation. But Bill was a hardened soldier five years my senior who had already been in combat. He was cordial with me when I asked him questions and sometimes advised me when he thought that he could be helpful, but he did not warm readily to others. Bill had already learned the hard lesson of integrating into a new unit. He kept to himself, within the limits of acceptable sociability, and soon melted into the background of the other strangers in the unit.

For the first time since stepping off the train in Leesville, Louisiana a year before, I was completely alone. Though by necessity the men of the unit were pressed together, the loneliness I felt was the result of my inherent resistance to the esprit de corps concept that had been ameliorated by my close friendships in flight school. I was thrown into the uncomfortable situation where the reality of a personal relationship had to be replaced with an abstraction that was supposed to inspire enthusiasm, loyalty and devotion to the group. Yet for me, without the intimacy of really knowing or caring for another individual, that kind of group dependency only made me feel more lonely and vulnerable.

We all understood the army's policy of one-on-one replacements in the combat zone. I suppose I had always known that, eventually, Mike and I would be separated, but I did not dwell on that eventuality. I even assumed that we would be together at Camp Evans in the same way that we had been together at An Khe. But Mike was living with his unit on the other side of the camp. He might as well have been on the other side of the country. Suddenly, like a hard slap in the face intent on waking me from an illusion, the reality of this war and the control that the military had over my life hit me.

By ordering a soldier here or there, the army could instantly shatter the intimacy carefully built between friends, destroying the sense of reality that grows out of one's vital attachments to other people. My need for that sense of reality was not an illusion that could be replaced with an abstract concept. For me, the reality of the war had to do with the evocation of the warrior spirit, which was much more important than conforming to the role of the mechanized soldier.

For most green recruits, the reality of combat was defined by an instinct for survival. But for the warrior spirit, reality meant focusing on the victory over death. The unexpected disorientation that came from being assigned to a field cot in a tent full of strangers distracted my focus, fragmented my energy and meant that, for me, the victory over death was no longer certain. It suddenly hit me that I was really going to miss my relationship with Mike.

My first night at Camp Evans I fell into a deep depression. Late in the night, I awoke and lay on my cot, holding my sleeping bag tightly around my face. The snores and grunts and muffled words of unremitting nightmares were the only sounds coming from my tent-mates in the opaque darkness, but large rats—our other companions in the tent—scurried across the floor, and I felt one scramble across my legs. I could not go back to sleep. For a long time I lay awake, trying to anchor myself in the fading memory of my relationship with Mike.

During WWII and the Korean War, a unit trained together and was assigned to combat as a single unit. Soldiers who bonded in their training could carry that bond into the combat zone. (The same has been true of soldiers in the wars in Iraq and Afghanistan.) But in Vietnam, the official policy replaced that "buddy system" with the abstract group spirit intended to inspire devotion and bring honor to the group. In that way, our war contrasted sharply with previous and present wars, and each soldier ended up fighting two wars at the same time: the enemy without and the demons of isolation within.

I was suddenly realizing that I would have to struggle with the demands of the warrior spirit alone. The initiation experience that Mike and I had shared throughout our training would not reach its conclusion until that kill-or-be-killed moment when my warrior spirit faced death. If I were to be victorious over death then, for the sake of my own sanity, I would need to share my victory with another, but Mike would not be there.

'To take a life is to act as an instrument of the gods,' I thought, for it is hubris to think that we, alone, can destroy an enemy. In other words, to triumph over death puts a tremendous burden on the soul, and the soul cries out to share that burden with a brother. I would soon see for myself, that time and again, in Vietnam, a soldier's first kill—his exalted victory over death; his climactic blood-right initiation into manhood—was celebrated in drunken loneliness.

Yet, in the combat zone there were stories of passionate fighters in whom the warrior spirit was fulfilled. Beyond the perimeter of our mechanized camp, wild Montagnard tribesmen fought on our side against the same enemy, sometimes using only the primitive weapons of spears and bows and arrows. While taking the life of an enemy served the abstract purposes of the government in Saigon and the American special forces teams that were working with them, to the Montagnard it was a fight between an oppressed people and their oppressors—a one-on-one confrontation, a simple battle between good and evil, between life and death.

Those fierce mountain dwellers were fighting to maintain their independent way of life. The victory over death was a reaffirmation of that life, to be shared in ecstatic celebration. Sometimes, or so I heard, victory was celebrated by cannibalizing the warm, still-pulsing heart of an enemy in order to magically assimilate the spirit of a valiant warrior. Initiated in his moment of triumph over death, the victorious Montagnard warrior was confirmed—by his intimate friends and by his community—as an instrument of the gods and resolved of moral guilt.

Thus the reality of the warrior spirit—at the moment when he confronts death at the hands of another warrior—is a deeply personal experience that transcends the military objective and political rationale of the fight. At that kill-or-be-killed moment, the enemy is death itself. Victory over death is the warrior's initiation into life, and his triumph needs to be shared in ritual affirmation.

The unrelenting conflict between my warrior spirit and the mechanized soldier that I was trained to be increased my depression, which was compounded by the fact that my first days in the war zone were routine and incredibly dull.

CHAPTER FIVE:

A Failed Initiation

During those first days, I only acted and reacted with the mechanized instinct of a modern soldier. Most of our missions were routine ash-and-trash missions, delivering mail and logistical supplies to outlying units from Camp Evans. I looked forward to those missions so that I could rise above the filth and clutter of the mechanized camp and drink, once more, of the majestic beauty of the landscape. The mountains, the sea and the land in between seemed a backdrop whose natural architecture gave a heroic dimension to the war. Yet no one talked of heroism or honor or glory. Such terms were considered self-aggrandizing. Instead, we talked of getting the job done. However, anyone should have begun to realize that "the job" was to serve as instruments of a political policy whose only measure of success was a body count and, therefore, whose only dictate to the soldier was, "Kill gooks!" It was a policy directive that did not take into account the complex emotions and finely tuned sensitivities inherent in the warrior's triumph over death.

The gooks had not been active for some time, and we anticipated a lull in the war in the form of another Tet cease-fire like the one President Johnson had ordered the year before. The lull gave me time to orient myself to the simple requirement of my own survival. But I noticed that the seasoned warriors were nervous, for there were whispered rumors throughout the camp—mostly derived from gut feelings—of a pending major offensive.

One quiet Sunday morning at the end of January, I was ordered to fly co-pilot with Doug, a short-timer with only two weeks left on his tour of duty. We were to fly one of the Hueys on a refueling mission to the Air Force base at Dong Ha near the capital of Quang Tri province. It was only about 30 miles from Camp Evans and a few miles south of the DMZ (the demilitarized zone that separated north and south Vietnam). Our own refueling station at Camp Evans was not yet fully operational and Major Frix had sent down orders to the aviation platoon that he wanted all of our aircraft fueled and combat ready. The Huey carried about three hours worth of fuel and our aircraft was down to about 30 minutes, a little more than enough fuel to get us to the Air Force base.

As aircraft commander, Doug flew. My duty as copilot was to scan the instruments and follow Doug lightly on the controls so that I could take over the aircraft if he was shot. We flew at a routine altitude of 5,000 feet because that put us out of range of small arms fire from the ground. As usual, our crew chief and a door gunner flew with us and, even though the M-60 machineguns on either side of the aircraft were armed and ready, both men sat relaxed in the back of the aircraft. Still enamored of the landscape, I took the opportunity to drink once more of its beauty.

Suddenly, my concentration was interrupted by several puffs of black smoke that appeared in the sky around us. I knew that they should not have been there, but I did not know what they were.

"My god, they're shooting at us with anti-aircraft guns. The gooks aren't supposed to have anti-aircraft guns!" Doug shouted nervously through the intercom, and his reaction was one of both surprise and fear. Every short-timer was extremely nervous about taking on even the most routine assignments and, after a year in Vietnam, Doug knew that the gooks had never had anti-aircraft weapons with which to threaten our superiority in the air.

We took evasive action. Doug pulled in power and increased our speed, twisting and turning through the sky as he maneuvered the Huey with the instincts he had learned flying scout missions. I followed lightly on the controls and scanned the instrument panel. Just then, an amber light flickered and began to glow, "We have a twenty-minute fuel warning," I informed him.

"Shit," Doug replied. "We can't get back to Evans and we'll never make it if we try to evade." Then, Doug dipped the nose of the aircraft forward, picked up speed and dove toward the earth. Flying "balls-to-the-wall" along the contour of the earth, skimming rice paddies, leaping over tree lines and praying that we wouldn't get hit, we headed straight for the Airbase at Dong Ha.

A few minutes from the airfield, I tuned the radio to the Air Force frequency and requested emergency landing instructions. The controllers voice crackled back into the earphones. "That's a negative, army chopper. We're under rocket attack. Hold and wait for further instructions."

"Like hell," Doug shouted nervously into the microphone. "We're out of fuel and we're coming in!"

We landed on the tarmac as close to a bunker as we could. A rocket exploded about a hundred yards to our left. We locked down the controls, shut off the engine and ran for shelter. Hunkered down behind sandbags, smoking cigarettes and talking nervously with the airmen with whom we shared the bunker, we listened intently to the series of explosions outside. The rocket attack lasted for another thirty minutes or so, and then all was silent.

When we dared to poke our heads out from behind the sandbags, we could see that, fortunately, the rockets had missed our helicopter. Eventually, we got our fuel and returned to Camp Evans.

The rocket attack on the Air Force base at Dong Ha was one of the most intense opening salvos of the Tet Offensive of 1968. In total, the Tet Offensive was a coordinated attack on 39 Provincial capitals, hundreds of towns and villages and the capital in Saigon.

The 1st Cav was thrown into the thick of the battle. In addition to the attack on the airbase, five battalions of NVA troops attacked the provincial capital of Quang Tri. Hué, the capital of *Thua Thien* province, was attacked by a contingent of 12,000 Viet Cong and regular troops from the North Vietnamese Army (NVA). They overran the Marines who were assigned to guard the airbase at Phu Bai, and they easily routed the small contingent of ARVN troops assigned to defend the nearby city of Hué. In the city itself, Viet Cong sympathizers had compiled a hit list of merchants, Buddhist monks, Catholic priests, intellectuals and others who supported the South Vietnamese government. NVA troops and Viet Cong moved house-to-house through the city executing some 3,000 civilians on that list, many in the doorways of their homes with their families looking on. It was one of the most horrific massacres of the war.

Three Marine battalions and a contingent of ARVN troops were sent to retake the city of Hué house-by-house and street-by-street in a battle that lasted for a month. The 1st Cav's job was to support them in the outlying areas. The 2nd Brigade successfully liberated the provincial capital of Quang Tri in ten days. My unit, the 3rd Brigade, was responsible for keeping Highway One open between those two provincial capitals. Thus, our primary operations, following the Tet Offensive, took place between the Airbase at Dong Ha and a small ARVN base north of the city of Hué called PK-17.

As the command and control unit for the brigade, we flew commanders back and forth between Camp Evans and PK-17. As the battle intensified, we flew increasingly more dangerous ash-and-trash missions to ground forces defending the transportation link and the area on either side of Highway One. Though 3rd Brigade troops were engaged in combat operations in one corner of the city and in outlying villages, we did not fly over Hué nor did we fly directly into that fight. As it turned out, for most of the month of February, the rainy season had begun in earnest and the sky remained lead-gray, with a low ceiling of cloud cover that severely restricted our flight operations.

Still, tension mounted with the intensity of each battle. During the day, there were constant troop movements in and out of the camp by truck and by helicopter. At night, there were frequent mortar and rocket attacks. The inevitable response salvos from our 105mm Howitzers shattered the stillness of the night with the flashing lights of explosions and ear-splitting thunder. In the weeks that followed the Tet offensive, I learned that nearly half of the pilots in my flight class—scattered in units all over Vietnam—had either been killed or wounded in action.

When Bob was killed, I was devastated. My reaction surprised me because we were never that friendly with each other. But his death brought to the surface all of the emotions that I felt—and had been keeping under control—over the separation of our foursome when we were sent to separate units, suddenly dissolving the bonds we had formed during our year of training.

The report we received was not official. It filtered down through the camp grapevine via word-of-mouth, a common practice whenever a comrade, another helicopter pilot, was killed. As such, the report picked-up, in the process, both judgments and innuendos slanted toward a condemnation of the cruelty and atrocities of the gooks. But this particular story also revealed the arrogance of one American officer in his handling of a certain type of combat situation.

Gunship pilots, like scouts, were the real warriors, set apart from the support units of transport aircraft, med-evac and command and control pilots by their aggressive participation in actual combat operations. Their job was to attack enemy strongholds or to lay down suppressing machinegun and rocket fire in support of advancing infantry. Bob was flying copilot on a routine gunship mission when his aircraft was shot down. The crew of four was unhurt, but they were captured by a small contingent of gooks. They were tied up and, while they were being led away, their captors were attacked by a single gunship commanded by an army major whose record for daring was unsurpassed in the division. However, this officer also had a reputation for being reckless and irresponsible. When attacked, the gooks used machetes to behead their captives and fled, unscathed, into the underbrush. That's how Bob was killed.

Logically, it would be hard to argue with the tactical position of the gooks. If aggressively attacked, our own troops, too, would very likely have killed their captives. We argued among ourselves about how we might have handled the situation, but we all agreed that the major's action was illogical. His decision to attack was either an unrealistic attempt to rescue the captives or simply a foolish miscalculation that cost four lives. Either way, his actions were taken without genuine regard for the lives of the prisoners. Those of us who knew Bob, the other pilot or the two crewmen were incensed by his disregard for the lives of our friends. We speculated on optional courses of action and how we might have reacted, had one of us been the major's copilot. But we all agreed that the major—who had already crashed several aircraft—was an arrogant, glory-seeking asshole who should have been grounded long ago.

Even if the events had been distorted in their grind through the rumor-mill, they stirred judgments about the arrogance of our leaders and questions about the soundness of command decisions. I was not yet completely oriented to the fight and still feeling vulnerable. So my confidence in the chain of command and my commitment to a higher purpose were important in providing me with a degree of psychological security. Now my confidence in the chain of command began to falter, and I questioned my commitment to seeking glory for myself and for our cause.

I imagined myself as the copilot of that glory-seeking major. Would my judgment have been less impulsive, sounder than his? I thought so. Yet while in the position of copilot, if I had questioned the command decision of a superior officer, I would have been at risk for a court-martial. The knowledge that superior officers were human and therefore fallible was not the issue. What disturbed me was being irrevocably locked into a system that bound in chains my power to make life-and-death decisions at the gut-level of my own warrior instinct. If the military's *follow-orders-without-question* mentality conflicted with the subjective dictates of the warrior spirit, then it would create a frustrating and life-threatening tension between military rigidity and the need to stay focused on the victory over death. No one knew that better than the infantry platoon sergeant who "fragged" some arrogant, glory-seeking, asshole lieutenant who was about to lead the platoon to its death just to prove that he was in charge.

My frustration was building toward the rage that fueled the warrior, but in camp I had to keep it under control. I maintained a cool, professional façade in my duties and a lonely distance from my fellow officers. I had not met another pilot in the unit to replace the bond I had shared with Mike, for everyone seemed to be locked-up in their own world. Though each of us dealt with his isolation in his own way, I suppose my way was perceived as aloofness and, therefore, a direct affront to the unit's esprit de corps. The official position was that questioning the esprit de corps affected morale. It did not take long for that situation to come to a head in a face-to-face confrontation with Al Eason, the self-appointed morale officer of our unit.

One evening I was lying on my cot reading. The tent was empty. All of the officers and NCOs were drinking together in another tent that served as our makeshift recreation hall. The drinking had become a nightly bonding ritual and, though I was not a real drinker, I had occasionally participated, without much enthusiasm. However, not to drink and socialize with one's comrades was considered an affront to the whole platoon. But on that particular evening I did not feel like participating at all.

Led by Al, a group of officers and NCOs suddenly burst into the officer's tent. Al was a heavy-set, blond Scandinavian with a ruddy complexion and a large handlebar mustache—the kind of man one might imagine in a lumberjack camp. He was a few years older than me and more robust and manlier than any of the other pilots. He was also more willing to prove his manliness by picking a fight under any convenient circumstances, especially when he was drunk. His cheeks and nose glowed red. Al was drunk.

He stood in front of the group, which mumbled threateningly as the tension and the bad vibration in the air increased, making me huddle more defensively into my sleeping bag and my book. But I lost my concentration entirely when I realized that their muttering was directed at me. They had successfully invaded my private space. It pissed me off. Now the fun could begin.

Al began to weave and stagger as he insulted me with his wobbly speech. "Hey, Mitch, you too fuckin' good to drink with us? Sittin' here readin' a book. Intellectual bullshit. Better than the rest of us? You mother-fucker! Come on! Get down off your super, superior fuckin' high horse and have a drink, you fuck."

I parried and fenced words across the tent with Al until my logic blundered and I ran out of responses to his insults. Then, I tried to withdraw. I was not very quick to understand their motives, which were probably driven by tension and boredom. I was only trying to maintain the integrity of my warrior spirit by staying aloof from the day-to-day routines of the mechanized soldier. Here was my first face-to-face confrontation as a warrior, and my rage was increasing in proportion to my confusion. The adrenaline pumped through my veins, making my body shake with anger at the absurd contradictions of the situation. Al and I were *supposed* to be on the same side.

Then I exploded. "FUCK YOU, EASON!!"

The rest of the group responded with a loud, "OOOH," as they realized that I had finally been provoked into a fight.

I jumped off the cot with my knees and arms shaking. In a travesty of a warrior's duel, Al and I faced each other down the long center aisle of the tent. Backed by his entourage of onlookers, Al threw back his head and laughed at me. But though I was furious, I had not lost my wits. I was not going to be goaded into a fistfight with Al.

Instead, I grabbed the magazine of my M-16 rifle that leaned against the wall of the tent next to my cot and pulled a round of ammunition from the chamber. Then I hurled the bullet toward him, wildly and furiously. It missed its mark, breaking a lamp instead, but the challenge was met, first with silence, and then with the *ooohs* and *aaahs* of the onlookers. We both armed ourselves with a handful of 7.62mm rifle bullets and hurled them at each other with unleashed fury, soliciting cheers from the crowd with each round that struck the opponent, leaving a red welt on the flesh that it did not have the power to penetrate.

Suddenly there was an explosion. Everyone scrambled.

A rocket had struck somewhere nearby and a siren screamed through the darkened camp. Ironically, the first confrontation with my warrior's passion was interrupted by the war. The whole incident did not dramatically change my attitude but, eventually, apologies were made and we all shook hands. Several days later the platoon commander, Captain Boyer, assigned me to fly copilot with Al, probably because he had heard about our confrontation and decided that flying together would be good for both of us.

We were flying a routine ash-and-trash mission delivering supplies to units in the field and had just landed to pick up some supplies when we heard a distress call. The radio call was relayed on the distress frequency from an Air Force jet flying overhead. It took me a minute to realize what was going on, but Al recognized immediately that the downed aircraft was one of our own. His focus sharpened like a javelin in flight, as he jotted down the coordinates and glanced at his map.

"Get that shit out of the aircraft!" he commanded, referring to the supplies we had just loaded. But the crew chief and door gunner were just as perplexed as I was. "Just push it out the door," he shouted. Then he turned to me, "They're only a few *clicks* (kilometers) from here. Stay sharp!"

Without hesitation, Al turned the Huey into the wind and pulled pitch. We had our bearings. The crash had occurred several kilometers from Highway One, directly west of the broken and rusting wreck of a Marine H-34 Choctaw helicopter that had been stuck in the mud for a couple of years and served as a perpetual landmark for those of us flying up and down the highway route. Al was a damn good pilot who had done his tour in scouts, and he was a valiant warrior. We flew low, keeping our eyes open for the wrecked Huey. I followed his every move on the controls while my eyes skimmed the control panel. "There she is," shouted the crew chief through the intercom.

The Huey was lying on its side in the middle of a huge, communal rice paddy, surrounded by a thick band of trees. The blades were shattered and the tail boom was broken in two. Still on the Air Force emergency frequency we were able to make contact with the crew of four that was hiding in the tree line. *"Be advised, there are hostiles in the area,"* was the warning we got over the radio, but Al had already decided on the strategy of surprise. We dove in low to the ground, dragging the toes of our skids through the grass at 125 miles an hour, then popped up over the tree line and flew directly over the wreck. We pulled sharply up into the sky. At about 300 feet, we ceased forward motion. Al executed a pedal turn that abruptly flipped the helicopter around 180 degrees, and we dove back down toward the wreck. Already, the crew was moving out of the tree line, running toward the center of the paddy. We landed. It was a complete surprise to the hostiles in the tree line that were looking for the crew of the downed aircraft. Then, they saw us and opened fire. Our door gunner and crew chief laid down suppressive fire from their M-60s. Just as the crew of four jumped on board, Fred, the pilot of the downed aircraft, got winged in the shoulder. We had landed into the wind. Al pulled pitch, and we were gone. I followed him lightly on the controls, called out readings on the instruments and kept a sharp eye out for landmarks because we were both a little bit disoriented and shaking from the adrenaline-rush. We climbed rapidly to 5,000 feet. Al shouted at me to give him a heading, and I scanned the landscape until I found a familiar landmark. None of us calmed down until we were safely back at the base.

Fred was med-evaced out to a medical unit, and the crew was debriefed on the incident. We later learned that there was an entire battalion of NVA regulars in that tree line looking for the crew of the downed aircraft. Al's quick thinking and faultless strategy saved the downed crew, as well as our own, from what could have been a disaster. Several days later, General John Tolson came down to the brigade headquarters and awarded the Silver Star to Al and a Distinguished Flying Cross to me and to our crew.

✡ ✡ ✡

In spite of the adrenaline-rush of such combat missions, the frustration grew inside me as my heartfelt warrior's passion conflicted with the outward role that I was expected to play. The lack of a close friend with whom I could vent my inner passion, and my growing awareness that the political objectives of the war always seemed to outweigh, and sometimes conflict with, the warrior's sense of morality weighed heavily on my spirit. Added to that was the fact that, after nearly six weeks in camp, I had not been close enough to the enemy to get to know him. But I learned to keep my attitude to myself and to force a more congenial façade with my colleagues. I played the role of the professional soldier that had been assigned to me and prepared for the confrontation with death as best I could.

Flying routine missions took me from small coastal villages to artillery emplacements in the hills. As I flew over the land, I could not help but marvel at the stands of bamboo, palm and the exotic fruit and flower-bearing trees that wound between the rice paddies and stood like sculpted barriers, dividing the land that yielded its wealth under the farmer's hand and plow. A wooden plow with a steel blade pulled by a water buffalo was the simple implement of a peasant people, farmers who tended the rice in the fields. They stood barefoot in calf-deep water, their bent bodies clothed in black pajamas with wide-brimmed conical straw hats protecting them against the intensity of the sun.

They did not look up when we flew over. Perhaps they had grown anesthetized to the daily routine of military activity. Or perhaps, fearful of death from the sky, they lowered their eyes to hide within the dark corridors of their souls any proclivities that would have made them seem suspicious to us. I saw them only as black figures against a landscape of green rice stalks that flowed back and forth in the downwash from the rotor blades as we flew over.

Perhaps in feature and personality they were not very different from the drafted country boys and urbanized non-coms that made up the corps of the ARVN forces with which we had frequent, limited contact when we flew in and out of PK-17. Those men spoke in a strange language. The language barrier alone was enough to separate them into *them* and *us.* But too, the cultural barrier was a wide chasm that gave us no other choice but to look at all the Vietnamese as being the same. Regardless of their individual social differences from each other, they were so culturally different in habit and mannerism from us that it challenged the engrained sense of our own American identity.

For example, the regular ARVN soldiers that fought with us did not seem to conform to our ideas of masculinity but moved as though their bodies had an inherent quality of suppleness that was almost effeminate. This presented a perpetual contrast to the tougher quality of their American-trained superior officers.

Too, their gestures and their way of relating to each other conveyed characteristic warmth that was objectionable to the hard, cold, emotionally detached attitude of the stereotypical American masculine image. While American soldiers made an effort to maintain a physical distance from each other, we often saw the ARVNs walking hand in hand or with their arms draped across each others shoulders or sleeping with their bodies curled up against each other on the floors of airports where they were awaiting transport from one front to another. They seemed to melt together in a patch of dark green uniform against a white tile floor, their eyes closed and their soft breathing coordinated in a rhythmic rise and fall of arms that lay across each other's chests.

I had never seen the ARVNs in battle but, when they were in camp together, they touched, laughed and teased each other like schoolboys. Their adolescent giddiness revealed the sensitivity with which they reached out to feel the movement of each other's bodies. Thus, they did not seem like hardened soldiers but more like immature copies of the mechanized soldiers that we were trained to be. That perceived immaturity did not come from their ages however—seventeen and up, much like the Americans—but from their peculiar, semi-primitive, agrarian culture that grew up out of the earth.

They were earth-warriors—progeny of the Goddess who ruled over the earth's vegetation and the Dragon King who ruled the rivers and the streams from his palace in the sea. That is what made them contrast so sharply with the sky-warrior image that we presented as we swooped down from the heavens, moving with lightening speed and precision from one front to another. I did not know what powers those earth-warriors possessed, but it made them different from us in a way that was both exotic and intriguing.

To judge the ARVN objectively, one would have to lay aside the idiosyncrasies of their personalities and see them only as soldiers in service to the same political objectives shared by our two governments. But in reality, the cultural differences made it impossible to be objective, and I found it impossible to be non-judgmental about the Vietnamese troops with whom I came in contact. The limited indoctrination I had been given made me feel as though all of the Vietnamese should first be arbitrarily labeled as the enemy. It was difficult to separate one from the other and say that because a man wore a dark green uniform, flew in American transports and also killed our mutual enemy that he, with his strange language and peculiar mannerisms, was essentially any different from a gook.

Weeks passed in which I learned no more about the enemy than those feelings of strangeness picked up by observing peasants from the air and the ARVN at PK-17. I skimmed over the countryside flying routine ash-and-trash missions, logging flight time. When the weather cleared enough so that we could go back to conducting command and control operations, I watched the war unfold from the surrealistic per-spective of an aerial command post. On those missions, we flew circles over the battlefield at 5,000 feet, watching men move over the ground like ants. Only soundless puffs of smoke indicated combat action. I could not hear the crack of rifle fire or the screams of men dying. I could not taste the blood or smell death or feel the passions of the warriors in battle. From that lofty perspective, it did not take long to become bored with the routine, and I was beginning to anticipate my rotation into scouts.

Though I was not supposed to fly scouts until I had been with the unit for four months, we had lost two of our best scout pilots during the first days of the Tet offensive and it only seemed logical that my turn was imminent. Ultimately, it would present the greatest challenge to both my sense of professionalism as a helicopter pilot and my warrior spirit.

The scout ships flew close to the ground and close to the action. They operated as scouts have always operated, moving slowly and stealthily ahead of the infantry, looking for the enemy, killing them when the opportunity presented itself and advising infantry commanders on enemy troop strength, movement and strongholds. The scouts were a two-man team, consisting of a pilot and an observer. They carried a skid-mounted .30 caliber machinegun controlled by the pilot from a trigger on the cyclic stick. The observer had his own arsenal of weapons: a door-hung 7.62mm machinegun, an M79 grenade launcher, an M16 rifle, a .45 caliber pistol and an assortment of hand grenades. They carried all the ammunition that the aircraft could carry and still fly.

It was a job that required both skill in flying and a honing of all the warrior's senses. As much as I looked forward to flying scouts as some kind of fulfillment of the warrior spirit, I was also filled with anxiety over the awareness that my passions were being suppressed by the sheer boredom and mechanical routine of our daily activities. I grudgingly accepted the fact that my training in the merger of man and machine had only instilled in me the proper instincts to *get the job done*. Secretly, I was no longer so confident. Each day I felt more enmeshed in the subtle network of controls that ran against the one element that insured the warrior's survival—the ability to passionately confront death. Routinely, I began to accept the army's supreme dominance over my duties, my career and my life. I started to have a foreboding feeling that flying the dangerous scout missions was a job too challenging for the mechanized soldier I was becoming. Like everyone else, I prayed to survive and waited for the day when I could go home. Still, flying scouts was the ultimate challenge, and I would not know if my warrior within could be unleashed until that challenge was met.

That conflict stressed my nerves and shocked my senses. It made me question *not* whether I had the courage to die for my country, but whether I had the courage to kill for my nation's passionless political objectives. If my warrior's passions were honed enough to be victorious over death, had I mastered myself enough to contain, for a lifetime, the memory of the death I would inflict on another without ritualistic celebration, without confirmation of my initiation into manhood, without the victory shared and acknowledged by my philos, Mike? Could I take the life of another without the assurance that I had mastered the moral creed of war as a conviction of honorable deeds, performed as a triumph of good over evil? When the cosmic duality of life and death came together, making me, for that moment in time, an instrument of the gods, would I be ready?

For those reasons, *'You need to know your enemy,'* were the words that resounded in my heart and in the deep unconsciousness of my dream space. But knowing the enemy seemed impossible because it was barred from my consciousness by the mechanized routine of our daily missions and by the security and controlled atmosphere of the camp where I lived. Then, finally, the opportunity came.

✧ ✧ ✧

Around the first of March, the American forces retook Hué. The 3rd Brigade became heavily engaged in mopping up operations in the surrounding countryside. I was flying copilot on a command and control mission for a battalion sweep of villages upstream, along the *Song Bo.* There were two villages that stood across a broad tributary from each other—one under the control of the communists and the other loyal to the South Vietnamese government. Since the beginning of the guerrilla war, a decade earlier, they had coexisted in a state of mutual tolerance. I did not know if the Tet offensive had changed that delicate balance, but I did know that the battalion commander we were working for that day had orders to sweep through the communist village on a search and destroy mission.

By the time the battalion moved in, all the men had fled the village with their families. Our troops swept through looking for arms' caches and chasing communists through the brush. On the orders of the lieutenant colonel who commanded the battalion and whose TOC was in the rear of our aircraft, we landed in the village. Then, my command pilot accompanied the battalion commander while he consulted with his ground troops. The crew chief and door gunner took care of the aircraft, and I was left with nothing to do.

Nearby was a farmer's hut. Actually, I reminded myself, he was a communist—a gook like the rest of the villagers: the enemy. With a casual, but nonetheless instinctive, concern for booby traps, like the ones we had learned about in An Khe, I wandered down a narrow path to the small clearing where the farmer's hut and work shed stood surrounded by a tall stand of bamboo. The stream gurgled quietly nearby. A bird chirped somewhere up in the bamboo trees, and in the distance the shouts of men at war could be heard.

I looked at the hut for a moment and, thinking that I might find a souvenir there, I carefully lifted the cloth that covered the doorway. I entered the man's home but instead of acquiring a souvenir, I discovered intimate details of my enemy's life.

The hut was a single rectangular room with bamboo walls, a dirt floor and a thatched roof. A double bed stood in one corner partitioned by a curtain that had been strung across the room. In the main part of the room there was another, smaller bed, perhaps for a child, and several other pieces of furniture. Above a bureau that stood against the far wall was a faded picture of an old woman—a matriarchal figure that I amusingly decided must have been the gook's mother-in-law. On top of the bureau a gently smoothed silk scarf, a half-burnt candle and several family relics seemed to form some kind of altar. I was touched by the indication of some form of ancestor worship, though I did not understand the man's motives or the significance of the objects that lay so delicately upon the scarf.

At the other end of the room, a stick fire still smoldered on a simple stone hearth. A few boxes and cans on a shelf above the hearth made a kitchen. That hearth conveyed the simplicity of the man's life. It was a well worn, flat, round stone with a depression in the middle where the fire was built. The stone was elevated above the dirt floor and leveled on several bricks, and there was a small stool in front of it for the one who tended the fire and cooked the meals. There was no chimney, and a sooty patch on the underside of the thatched roof indicated where the smoke seeped through.

Though I had started this venture looking for something to steal, I looked around without touching anything. I had been warned that there might also be booby traps in the house, but in my heart I had a simple respect for the property of this man, this gook who had suddenly acquired flesh and blood and a living personality. I suppose I stood there for about five minutes inspecting the empty silence of the man's home. I wanted to feel his presence, but he had escaped with his phantoms, leaving me only some household relics with which to speculate on his identity. Then I turned, carefully lifted the cloth and went back out into the yard.

There were no animals, though bits of feathers stirred in the dust by the wind indicated that there had been at least one scrawny chicken, and prints on the ground looked like those of a dog. The ground was bare dirt, except for clumps of grass that grew where the vertical bamboo walls of the hut touched the ground. The curtains over the door and the window moved with a wisp of air that also rustled and twisted the fringes of the thatched roof. The faint sound of the wind blowing intermittently through the vegetation played an eerie counterpoint to the silence.

It made me feel strange, standing there in my olive drab fatigues, my combat boots, my flack vest and the spherical flight helmet that I held in the crook of my arm. I was an over-sized hulk of a man, compared to the dimensions of the house and the clearing that had been cut to fit the smaller frame of the Vietnamese peasant to whom it belonged. There, I was the stranger: the out of place figure. At that moment, more than ever before, I felt not the strangeness of Vietnam but how incongruent I seemed in that environment. For in that small clearing of bamboo, surrounded by the war, there existed a feeling of peace—the first moment of peace I had felt since Mike and I sat in the restaurant in An Khe and I made my first eye contact with the Vietnamese in the person of a pretty little girl in a pink dress. My nerves relaxed and I felt my heart beat softly. My breathing released a month of tension, rising and falling with a serene rhythm that emanated from a barely perceptible vibration in the air. I stood for what seemed like a long time, drinking in that feeling and just staring at the wall of bamboo trees that surrounded me. Then, my gaze focused on the work shed.

I did not immediately move to investigate, because my feet felt so solid on the ground, connecting me to the earth and to the peacefulness of that place. Then, the muffled shouts of soldiers and the distant crack of a rifle shot brought back the reality of the war. I sighed deeply, released what was left of my paranoid sense of caution and walked toward the shed. I simply knew that the warning against booby traps did not apply, for this was not the kind of man to shatter his own peaceful setting with explosive destruction. I amused myself with the thought that it would not be in the character of a man who worshiped his mother-in-law.

I had been staring at an object that projected perhaps fifteen feet beyond the open side of the shed. As I got closer, I realized that it was a waterwheel. The hand-made mechanism had an elongated arm with a gear at each end, containing a double row of bamboo cups attached to a bamboo chain. I had never seen anything like it before, and I inspected it carefully. The cups were segments cut from thick bamboo trees, and each cup was about ten inches deep and five or six inches in diameter. The cups were fixed onto a bamboo assembly that was really a combination conveyor-belt and chain. It had a gear wheel at each end and this, in turn, was supported on the frame. The entire mechanism was made of bamboo. Where pieces were joined together, holes had been drilled and carefully carved bamboo pegs inserted. The complete mechanism was over twenty-five feet long. It stuck out of the shed on a diagonal, angled upward to a height of about ten feet, and this gave me a clue as to how it worked.

The waterwheel was moved to the edge of the stream on four wooden wheels. The lower end was set in the water and the conveyor/chain assembly was moved so that the cups scooped up the water. The incline of the elongated arm was such that the water did not spill until the cups rounded the upper end of the conveyor. Then, each cup descended, inverted, back down to the stream. By inspecting the mechanism to see how it was operated, I discovered a small-toothed metal gear. The waterwheel, it seemed, could be operated with a bicycle simply by removing the rear wheel and attaching the bicycle chain to the metal gear.

This was technology. Like everything else I had encountered in rural Vietnam, the technology was primitive, but it displayed imagination and ingenuity, with an uncanny faculty for adapting the materials and mechanisms at hand to the work to be done. The contraption contrasted sharply with my own experience of technology, but it also made me realize that it did not matter that this farmer had no sophisticated pumping equipment. Considering the size of his plot of land, his simple country life did not need to be usurped by automation. Then, in my imagination, I began to conjure a vision of the man who had built this contraption.

This man—this gook—may have said to his wife, "Today, I water the field." With the help of his neighbors, and perhaps a neighbor's water buffalo, the mechanical contraption was pulled to the stream along narrow paths lined with the overarching boughs of bamboo trees. He gave directions to his neighbors in the singsong, heavily accented peasant idiom of his native tongue. Then, he threw back his head and laughed, his dark eyes squinting into the bright glare of the morning sun, his lips pulled back over large teeth that protruded slightly and gave his features a characteristic country look. He was happy, for this was his day.

His neighbors followed his instructions as he had followed theirs on other days, and the waterwheel was positioned in the stream that ran beside his field. The stream flowed very slowly, and he noted that it would allow him to pump a great deal of water. The small field needed two or three inches of water. That meant that he would spend all day on his bicycle and, in return for his day's labor, he would have a good crop to harvest—enough to feed his family and to give the soldiers their quota.

He did not think of politics. The village elders decided what was best for the village and, because this was his home and his land, he would do as they wished. In fact, if he had lived on the other side of the stream his life would have been much the same, tending his field and raising his family. The leaders of both villages told propaganda lies. The man who lived across the stream had neither more land nor a better life.

He set to work on his bicycle with his back to the neighbor across the stream with whom he had never spoken face to face. But he was not concerned with danger. Yes, there had been violence between the two villages during the years of warfare when each village had allied itself with a different political system. Some men had been killed, and the boys still fought each other when they went to bathe in the stream, coming by chance to the same bathing spot. But today, the gook's only concern was to pump enough water for his crops, and he had found the rhythm to keep the buckets flowing smoothly along the conveyor assembly of his waterwheel.

At noon, his wife came to the field with a bowl of rice and some fish. She wore the traditional black silk pajamas of peasants. Her feet shuffled along the path in her simple sandals and her long black hair streamed down her back beneath the conical straw hat that shielded her face from the sun. She carried the bowl in her cupped hands, her face down and her eyes on the path. She had worked that morning in the house and would spend the afternoon working in the field while her husband continued to pump water.

I mused at the textbook images that flowed through my mind painting an imaginary portrait of my enemy. Was he, indeed, as simple as I imagined? I accepted the vision, for never before in my experience had I encountered peasants—people whose simple existence hugged the earth that nourished them. Certainly, it was there that his allegiance lay, with the land, and not with abstract political systems. What was most important to this man was what he raised—a crop and a family. The family depended on the crop, and the crop depended on the cycle of the seasons, the rains in the mountains and the benevolent Earth Mother and gods who kept pestilence and the ravages of war away from his tiny field.

As for the village government that was aligned with the communists against the repressions of the regime in Saigon, perhaps it also ensured that he could work the same field as his father before him and, perhaps, even provided him young rice seedlings from a communal stock. Perhaps, too, he was particularly sensitive to the communal effort required to insure the survival of the whole village. For those reasons, he may have agreed with the form of government that the village elders had chosen. Had he not agreed, he could have left his home and joined the ARVN forces.

His part in the war, however, was not to fight for a political ideology, but to defend his land and his home, to defend his intricate allegiance to the forces of nature that provided him with a livelihood and a reason for being. Many like him had lost those allegiances, lost their homes, lost their families, lost their lives. Like him, they did not follow the dictates of challenging intellectual controversies but only the propaganda slogans of their leaders and their own instinct for survival. That instinct, like my own, could easily be molded to the intricate purposes of whatever socio-political machinery determined his destiny.

Our warlords had shaped my allegiance to the warrior spirit. The peasant's allegiance, I imagined, was to the land—the rich, green earth between the mountains and the sea that formed the boundaries of his world. But he was also loyal to an ancient memory of the origins of his people, his world and his culture—the memory of the Goddess from the 36th heaven, the Sea Dragon and other deities drawn from Buddhism, Catholicism and Animism, blended into a religion that revered life. The seedlings from which he grew his crop were sacred, and offerings to the gods were taken from the crops. Flower petals were thrown into the stream as a reverent gift to the Dragon King who made the clouds and the waters that flowed to the sea, and prayers for rain were carried on the songs of the people in memory of Au Co's tears. Those prayers were projected into the ethereal realm where both the gods and demons dwelt.

Were we, in his simple peasant mind, the demons? We swept down from the sky not bringing rain but raining fire that devastated homes and crops—fire that came from the droppings of enormous silver birds that streaked like lightening across the sky. Those droppings plummeted down through the clouds with a shrill whistle and an explosive force that blasted away the velvety green covering of the nourishing earth and left it barren and poisonous.

Were we those demons? For we were mechanized soldiers whose only announcement of arrival was the terrifying "whop, whop" sound of rotor blades shattering the air above the tree line, mechanized soldiers whose machines were so sophisticated that they defied the imagination of a simple people whose consciousness accepted them as mechanical constructs but whose dream-vision saw them as monsters that disgorged death and destruction on the land of which the peasants were a part.

Was I one of those demons? For I was the control unit of a mechanical monster that hovered a few feet above the ground, a monster with twin Plexiglas bubbles that looked like a pair of eyes slung beneath wings that thrust the wind against the earth and pointed long, black metal fingers that spit death. Inside, I sat rigidly at the controls, clothed in armor with a huge, shiny, round helmeted head whose dark green window hid the human feature of my eyes. Was I, in the peasant's eyes, only an instrument of death?

I looked down at the spherical shell of the flight helmet that I held in the crook of my arm and moved the visor up and down, watching the reflection of the waterwheel appear and disappear as the visor slid back into its housing.

What would happen now to the man who had built that waterwheel? Would he be forced to join the guerrillas? His survival skills and his dexterity were verified by the success of his simple existence, but did they include the skills of an earth warrior? Would he go to a camp somewhere in the mountains to be trained to kill? Would his allegiance be transferred from the defense of his home and land, to the defense of an abstract political doctrine that now controlled his life in a whole new way? Perhaps he would form an allegiance to the god of war, as I had done. Still, I could not imagine that he would break so completely with the earth as to become a mechanized soldier. No, he would remain an earth warrior and, like the ARVN forces, he would remain true to himself, to the inherent sensuality and softness that emanated from the earth, his first true allegiance. What power and ferocity that would give him as a warrior I did not know, for I did not know the earth deities or how they gave, to their own, the courage and strength to defend the land against the demons from the sky.

Again, I ran my hand over the smooth surface of the waterwheel's frame, feeling the strength of the joints that were pegged with bamboo and tied with vines. The conveyor assembly was supple and moved in my hand, causing the gears at both ends to turn with a squeaking noise that shattered the silence of the clearing. This piece of machinery, primitive yet both strong and supple, was like the man I would face in battle.

Then I knew in my heart that he would defeat me. He would defeat me because he was certain of his strength and because he could bend and adapt more easily than me, like the suppleness and strength he had built into his waterwheel. He would defeat me because he was certain of the deities he defended, and because he would go into the battle with the boyhood friends with whom he had bathed in the river. He would defeat me because he could share with them, without moral shame, the triumph of life over death. And he would defeat me because the warrior's creed emblazoned in his peasant heart told him to stand firm and defend his home.

And after he defeated me, all his warrior passions would subside, and he would return to raise his crops and his family and show reverence to the deities that ruled over his life. The government to which he would swear allegiance would make as little difference in the future as it had in the past.

Just then, my crew chief burst into the clearing to announce that we were ready to leave. I pulled on my leather gloves and followed him back down the path. A young lieutenant, accompanied by a soldier with a flame-thrower, walked passed us toward the clearing. As I strapped myself into the copilot's seat, I could see thick curls of black smoke rising above the bamboo—the hut, the shed and the waterwheel offered as a sacrifice to the god of war.

✲ ✲ ✲

We returned to Camp Evans, throwing a vortex of dust into the air when we touched down on our hilltop landing-pad. Capt. Boyer had given instructions by radio that I was to see him when we returned from the mission. He told me that, in addition to my regular duties, I would begin spending at least two hours a day practicing scout maneuvers with the OH-13 scout ship, in the dunes beyond the perimeter of the camp. I was required to have a minimum of ten hours transitional training time to become familiar with the flight characteristics and maneuverability of the aircraft before flying scout missions, and he assured me that I would get it. But with two of our three scout pilots, Flanagan and Francione, in the hospital and only one scout pilot left in the unit, he needed to have another scout pilot trained and available as soon as possible, and I was up next for the job.

Our unit was still short of both aircraft and manpower. A week before the Tet Offensive started, Flanagan and Francione had been sent to Tan Son Nhat Airbase in Saigon to pick up a new OH-6 *Cayusa* aircraft that was going to replace the OH-13s as our primary scout ship. They spent a week of training, learning the flight characteristics of the new aircraft, and left Saigon on Saturday to fly the OH-6 up to Camp Evans—a two-day trip. Early Sunday morning they decided on a whim to fly under the bridges over the Perfume River in Hué. What they didn't know was that it was the first day of the Tet Offensive, and that NVA troops happen to be marching across those bridges as they approached them. They were attacked. The aircraft received twenty bullet holes, and a .50

caliber machinegun round that passed through the door of the aircraft also passed through both legs of both pilots. It was only a flesh wound, though it left them bleeding profusely as they flew the aircraft to Camp Evans. Both pilots were then med-evaced out of the war zone. That left us with only one pilot to fly scout missions.

But anyway, we could barely keep our two remaining scout ships in the air. The OH-6 was damaged beyond repair and one of the two remaining OH-13s needed more extensive repairs than Bill could manage. He carried that ship in a sling beneath one of the Hueys to the Airbase at Da Nang. The OH-6s were not fully deployed, and a new replacement OH-13 was on the way.

After the weather cleared, the whole camp seemed to be buzzing with activity. The division had begun an offensive sweep of the villages around Hué, like the mission from which I had just returned. Too, there were already rumors throughout the camp of a mission to rescue the Marines who were pinned-down at Khe San—a mountain valley some fifty or sixty miles to the northwest of Camp Evans. Now that the division was on the move, we all became much more aware of troop strength and of the number of losses incurred during Tet.

I inquired about Mike and was relieved to hear that he had survived the Tet offensive, though his unit had been heavily involved in dangerous, low level flights transporting troops throughout our area of operation. I wanted desperately to see him. But when we met it was without the warm feelings that had previously characterized our friendship. I had steeled myself to the new requirements of integrating into my unit and understood that he had probably done the same. Still, I wondered if he had made new friends more easily than me. Or perhaps he had resolutely blocked-out all sentiments as a concession to the requirement of survival.

We talked about Bob, trying to remind each other of fonder times during our training. When I told Mike that I was transitioning into scouts and anticipating my first kill, it was with false bravado, a failed attempt to invoke my unrequited desire to share that experience with my philos, but even that was gone. The conversation turned to survival. With most of the feeling drained from our relationship by the distance that the war put between us, we parted, wishing each other luck in the battle just to stay alive.

In the following days, I worked hard. I flew command-and-control missions six or seven hours a day, then spent two hours alone in the late afternoon practicing scout maneuvers with the OH-13. During those practice session, I thought of nothing but my proficiency with the aircraft. Most of all, I tried not to dwell on the fact that I was rapidly losing my enthusiasm for the adventure of war. I mustered my courage by grading myself on my technical proficiency, even practicing the dangerous maneuver of making a 360-degree turn with only the toe of one skid touching the ground. A master pilot could do it leaving a perfect circle in the dust no more than a foot in diameter.

As the weather continued to improve, each day more calls were coming in from field commanders requesting scout missions. Even with Flanagan and Francione out of commission and in the hospital, Capt. Boyer could not turn them all down. While some of the less daring missions were taken, reluctantly, by pilots who had already served their time in scouts and moved on to become aircraft commanders in the Hueys, most of the scout missions fell on the shoulders of our one remaining scout pilot.

Steve was an excellent pilot who already had several months' experience flying scouts. He had killed his quota of gooks and was getting nervous over the law of averages that pitted his warrior skills against the survival rate of scout pilots. During our evening drinking sessions in the tent that served as our unit clubhouse, he and the other scouts—the observers—kept mainly to themselves, as though the pressure of being real warriors set them apart from those of us whose piloting duties seemed routine by comparison. Only our best observers—a couple of sharpshooter mountain boys from West Virginia—bragged about scouting. They maintained a rivalry over their number of confirmed kills, sometimes arguing for hours about the gook in the bushes whose leg was still twitching as the scout ship turned into the wind and flew away.

Sometimes they would call Steve into the argument, but he waved them off to show that he could not be coerced into talking about the blood on his hands. He struggled silently and alone with his initiation into manhood. As I observed him, I could see that his nerves were edging toward the breaking point. We both knew that I was the relief that he was waiting for. Though we rarely spoke with each other, we sensed the bond between us—the knowledge that I would soon take his place and perhaps received the bullet that had his name on it: the one he saw in his dreams and visions waiting *out there* among the gooks.

I could see that with each new mission Steve seemed to struggle with an internal tension that threatened both his courage and his sanity. Since he was the only active scout pilot left in our unit, he did have the rare luxury to accept a mission or turn it down. But upon accepting it, he could not know what waited for him on the field of battle nor share with others his lonely confrontation with death.

Then, one day, he did share that strain with all of us, directly from the field by radio. Practically the whole platoon was gathered in and around the communications tent, as Steve's voice came crackling over the radio with increasingly violent agitation. The prerogative of his warrior spirit had faltered, and he demanded to speak directly to the brigade commander.

Steve had encountered a man walking on a dike between two rice paddies. As Steve described him, he wore the traditional sandals, black pajamas and conical straw hat of a typical peasant. He was an old man with long, white hair braided into a pigtail and a thin white beard that streamed down onto his chest from his sun-darkened and wrinkled face. Steve had flown to a point behind the old man, who turned to face the demon from the sky with clear unflinching eyes.

Steve hovered the aircraft three feet above the ground in front of the old man while the observer, Olson, leaning half-out of the helicopter door, pointed his M-16 at the old man and ordered him to place his hands on top of his head. The old man's hat was blown off by the wind from the rotor blade, and he squinted his dark eyes against the dust. Olson, whose orders came from Steve over the aircraft intercom, lowered his rifle so he could conduct the interrogation with hand signals and a few words of Vietnamese, while Steve kept the black, perforated barrel of this skid-mounted .30 caliber machinegun pointed at the old man. Olson told the old man to lift his shirt, and the old man complied. Then Olson ordered the old man to drop his pants, to see if he was concealing a weapon. The old man shook his head in a firm, "No!" and there the stalemate began.

We all listened as Steve first briefed Captain Boyer and then the company CO, Major Frix, his voice growing more riddled with tension at each passing moment. Steve would have to turn the tail of the aircraft toward the old man in order to take off into the wind. If the old man was concealing a weapon, one well placed round could bring the aircraft down, possibly killing Steve and Olson. But as the stalemate continued, Steve seemed more convinced that the old man was only stubbornly protecting his pious, country modesty, defying the will of the monster and its demon pilot that hovered in front of him.

The problem was that our area of operation was a tactical "free-fire" zone. Everything that moved was subject to interrogation, and resisting interrogation meant getting "wasted." All the locals knew that. Still, it was evident that Steve did not want to kill the old man. Perhaps he already had too much blood on his hands, or his stomach turned at the thought of an uncontested killing, an outright murder, a crime against man and God. But even though Steve knew those things, he was caught up in the grip of fear. He dared not turn the aircraft and fly away. And with every passing moment, the hungry fires of the engine drained his tanks of precious fuel. A decision had to be made, but Steve would not kill the old man without a direct order from the brigade commander.

Colonel Campbell had been summoned. As he walked through the crowd assembled at the mouth of the tent, he was obviously disturbed at having been called away from lunch with his battalion commanders. The colonel was impeccably dressed in crisp, starched fatigues with black eagles sewn to the collars. A man of perhaps forty years, his silver hair was smoothed back along the sides of his head, just long enough to reach his shirt collar. He had a trim, silver mustache and steel-blue eyes that accented his well-tanned face. Major Frix had briefed him on the way to the communications tent.

Steve was shouting, his voice cracking with tension. The radio operator tried to calm him by telling him that the colonel had just arrived. Colonel Campbell picked up the microphone and confirmed his identity. Steve, recognizing Campbell's voice, acknowledged. Then, Campbell turned calm and icy cold. "Mister, you kill that son-of-a-bitch right now or you're going to face a court martial!"

The tent fell silent as everyone listened for Steve's reply. Holding back the emotion in his voice as best he could, Steve replied with a crisp, "Yes, sir." Then he left the microphone key open so that we all heard the burst of fire from the .30 caliber machinegun.

The colonel keyed his microphone again. "Well done, soldier. Return to base." He put down the microphone, and we cleared a path for him as he strode out of the tent.

Some of us went to the landing pad to watch the eastern sky for Steve's aircraft. We each harbored an unspoken compassion but still could not find the strength to break through the facades of our professional egos and express, even among ourselves, the deep emotions that we shared with Steve.

When he landed, Steve stepped out of the aircraft and threw his helmet to the ground with tremendous rage. Making no effort to hide the tears that streamed down his cheeks, he turned his face to the sky with a look of pain marked by the flickering shadows of the still turning rotor blade. He fought off every attempt at being consoled, and he defied a direct order to report to Captain Boyer for a debriefing. Instead, he went directly to the chaplain's tent where he refused, under any circumstances, to ever fly scout missions again. As far as the unit was concerned, there would be a one-for-one trade off. I only had two hours left on my transition. The following morning, I would be the scout pilot.

☆ ☆ ☆

The dawn came with a clear golden light and a crisp blue sky that, with the end of the rainy season, we had come to expect. Steve had not left the sanctuary of the chaplain's tent, and I had orders to complete my transition immediately. I went to the landing pad, strapped the aircraft to my back and took off for my practice area.

That morning I practiced autorotations. Thoughtless, effortlessly, instinctively, I flew the aircraft upward in a graceful spiral to 5,000 feet, closed the throttle to idle, bottomed the collective stick to minimize lift on the rotor blades and dropped out of the sky at a rate of 2,000 feet per minute. At fifty feet, I flared the aircraft to slow my speed. At eighteen feet, I "popped pitch" by pulling up sharply on the collective stick to arrest my fall. At three feet, I eased-in the remaining blade pitch and set the aircraft gently on the ground. Again, I revved up the engine, took off, climbed and dropped, over and over again, feeling the vibrations of the aircraft in my back, butt and thighs where I was strapped securely to the machine, merging myself and my anxieties with the insensitive mass of Plexiglas and metal; burying within myself the desperation I felt so that I could become an emotionless, efficient control unit—an attitude that would either ensure my survival or make me a justifiable homicide in the peasant warrior's struggle with the demons of the air.

Those last two hours of my transition time were consumed, simultaneously, with the gasoline in my fuel tanks. I returned to the camp, landed and refueled. Already, I had received orders by radio for my first scout mission.

I was to fly into the ridge of mountains where the Song Bo flowed through a deep gorge and pick up Captain Miles, an infantry company commander. I located the coordinates of the landing zone (LZ) on my map and traced the route I would fly—southwest to the river then follow it into the mountains at an altitude of 5,000 feet above the ground. The LZ was on a high, narrow spit of land at a sharp horseshoe bend in the river. Miles' company had been flown in that morning with orders to sweep the area. He wanted to make an aerial reconnaissance before moving his infantry units.

I knew Captain Miles. We had been through the orientation at An Khe together, and I felt more secure knowing that my first scout mission was also to be a reunion with an acquaintance. On this mission, I did not have the .30 caliber machinegun mounted to the skid. We would be flying high above the ground, and I had no intention of drawing fire. It was a simple reconnaissance mission. I had only to follow his orders on the areas he wanted to observe and to stay within both the range of my proficiency and the limitations of the aircraft.

I flew toward the wall of mountains with confidence and, as I passed through the gap where the river flowed, I spotted the hilltop LZ. I had never flown that far into the mountains before, and the landscape was more dramatic than any I had experienced on the coast. The slope of the far riverbank rose dramatically, nearly two thousand feet, to a rocky pinnacle. It was covered with lush green foliage that made the steeply rising wall, soft, virgin and natural, though it also occurred to me that it was good cover for a sniper. Still, my spirit was uplifted by the grandeur of the landscape, and I felt lucky to have the privilege and power to fly over it with the confidence that I was in complete control of my machine. At that moment I was not thinking of my helicopter as a monster of war and myself as its guiding demon. On this mission, while Miles studied the topography for its military value, I could just observe the magnificence of God's handiwork.

I circled the LZ at 5,000 feet, waiting for a logistic supply ship to depart, for it was a small LZ with room for only one aircraft at a time. Then I cut the throttle to idle and dropped out of the sky in a graceful spiral. Only this time I maintained enough forward speed to bring back power at about 200 feet above the ground and finesse my aircraft into a gently descending glide path that brought me to a three-foot hover over the center of the LZ. The maneuver was perfectly executed. The problem, however, was to set the aircraft on the ground, which sloped down to my left. The Hueys that had delivered the troops and the Huey that had just departed had little difficulty settling on the ground because that aircraft had a wider skid-base and could land more easily on the slope. The OH-13 was smaller and more limited on slope landings. I proceeded with caution.

The company radio operator sat on the ground about twenty yards in front of me. I explained that the landing was going to be tricky and asked to speak with Captain Miles, but he could not be found. Cautiously, I descended, letting the upslope skid rest on the ground while I slowly lowered the down-slope, left skid. Then a gust of wind rocked the aircraft. I pulled pitch so that the right skid hovered about a foot above the ground.

At that moment, Miles emerged from beyond the limits of my peripheral vision and jumped onto the right skid. His 220 pounds of mass, multiplied by the velocity of his jump, created an incredible amount of destabilizing force that was thrown, suddenly and uncontrollably, into the delicately balanced equation that kept the fuselage of my helicopter suspended beneath the rotor disc. It was an incredibly stupid miscalculation on the part of Captain Miles.

The right skid hit hard against the ground. I struggled to regain control, and the aircraft leaned too far to the left. But already recovery was impossible. The impact had ruptured a fuel line and, at that moment, the cockpit was engulfed in a ball of fire. I was in the left seat and did not want to be pinned on the down-slope side. I threw the cyclic control stick hard to the right to force the aircraft to the ground on the up-slope side, opened the latch on my shoulder-waist harness and lost consciousness.

Later, they told me that a young lieutenant had pulled me from the wreckage and, miraculously, was not burned. But I knew that it was my Guardian Angel disguised as an army officer.

Two or three minutes later, on the ground about ten yards from the aircraft, I regained consciousness, not knowing how I had escaped the inferno that was consuming the twisted and tortured scrap of metal and Plexiglas that had been my flying machine. A medic squeezed a tube of morphine into my veins, while someone cut the gloves from my burned and rapidly swelling hands. I looked back at the aircraft, my eyes riveted on the flames that licked at the recently filled fuel tank. "She's gonna blow," I yelled, and we all got up and ran another twenty yards from the crash. Then, I collapsed in uncontrollable sobs, my entire body racked with pain. Most of my clothes had been burned away and the skin on my arms and legs had turned charcoal black, swelling, cracking and hissing with steam. The flack vest had protected my torso, and the helmet had protected my head. But my face, too, was severely burned and began to swell.

The medic cut away what was left of my clothes, wrapped my body in field bandages and treated me for shock. I fluctuated between uncontrollable fits of hysterical sobbing and periods of clear, lucid calm. A med-evac helicopter had been called, but it would have to wait for the fire to burn out before it could land in the small LZ.

It was more than an hour after the crash when I arrived at the field hospital at Camp Evans. Again, my wounds were dressed, and I could see the extent of the third-degree burns that covered forty percent of my body. But most of all, I was afraid of losing consciousness, fearing that it would be the moment of death. Later that afternoon, I was flown to the Airbase at Da Nang and transferred to a large Marine CH-47 Chinook helicopter with about twenty other wounded soldiers. We were flown to the USS Sanctuary, a hospital ship located a few miles off the Vietnam coast, and I was placed in the intensive care ward.

Though I was full of drugs, I could not sleep for fear of the Angel of Death that reached out for my warrior spirit each time I closed my eyes. Then late in the night, when all was dark and still, buzzers sounded and a red light flashed. Painfully, I rolled my head to the side to investigate. Nurses and a doctor dressed in white flashed by me to the side of another wounded soldier whose bed was in front of mine. The doctor placed the round pads of the defibrillator against his chest. Once. Twice. Three times, I listened to the "thud" of the electric charge as it passed through his heart. Then, silence. A white sheet was pulled over his face, and the doctor and the nurses quietly disappeared, leaving me alone with the dead.

The Angel of Death had turned his emaciated face away from me and pointed his bony finger at the other as if to say to me, *your time has not yet come.* He made his choice and left me to survive the war in Vietnam. I rolled my head back toward the wall. Tears that I could not wipe away with swollen hands rapped in gauze soaked the bandages that covered half my face. I said a silent prayer for my brother-in-arms and closed my eyes to sleep.

CHAPTER SIX:

Coming Home

It was embarrassing to have crashed, to have to admit to myself that the only adversaries my warrior spirit had confronted in Vietnam were Al Eason's defense of unit morale and Captain Miles' failure to follow proper procedure with the helicopter. (Miles escaped the incident unscathed.) I was tormented consciously by the embarrassment, but I was even more tormented by my failed initiation. I had imagined that the only way to complete my initiation into selfhood—to gain mastery over myself—was to meet death in a face-to-face, blood-right confrontation with another warrior. Confronting death in a helicopter crash left my initiation in limbo and, unless I could return to the war, it would never be completed. That realization threw me into a suicidal depression, and I cursed and blasphemed the Dark Angel that had embraced the other and let me live.

In the intensive care ward of the USS Sanctuary, my injuries were stabilized with painkilling drugs and antibiotics. Both my legs and both my arms were completely wrapped in white gauze, and my face was bandaged. Only the tips of my fingers emerged from the gauze bubbles around my hands. After two days, I was sent back to Da Nang, placed on an Air Force transport with a number of other wounded troops and shipped to the naval hospital at Subic Bay in the Philippines where I stayed for another two days. My burns were washed and swabbed with sulfur-based creams to prevent infection and re-bandaged.

From Subic Bay, I was sent to the 106th General Hospital in Yokohama, Japan where doctors began the first series of treatments.

The tedious and painful procedure was called "debridement," which involved pulling the dead, burned skin away from the raw muscle tissue with tweezers and carefully cutting it away with surgical scissors. Again, the raw muscles and nerve fibers were swathed in antibiotic sulfur creams to prevent infection. I was once more packaged in white gauze and given a numbing cocktail of painkilling drugs.

After two weeks in Japan, I was loaded onto an Air Force transport with a dozen other burn patients for the long trans-pacific flight, via California, to San Antonio, Texas. We were driven from the airfield by ambulance, wheeled on gurneys into the army's Burn Center at Brooke General Hospital, Fort Sam Houston and greeted by a dozen doctors and nurses from the staff. The Chief Surgeon inspected each of us, one at a time. He looked at the severity of my burns, marked his clipboard and pronounced his professional opinion of my injuries. I heard him say to the other doctors without emotion, "We'll have to remove both his legs." Though I was conscious, the painkillers made me giddy, and the news made me want to laugh. I had an absurd vision of rolling my severed body along on a wooden platform tied to four roller skates. At the same time, I wanted to cry.

But, once again, my Guardian Angel interceded. A young doctor stepped in. "Let me have this one. I'll see what I can do to save his legs." The Chief Surgeon agreed, and I was wheeled off to the burn ward.

My legs were not amputated. Slowly, the weeks of doctors and nurses, bedpans and the aseptic smell of the burn ward turned into months of surgical procedures, healing and recovery. The less severely burned areas of my body healed on their own, and pink patches of new skin appeared under the scabs on my face, my hands and my elbows. The remaining seared flesh on my arms and legs was removed. Then began the slow and tedious procedure of skin grafting. A layer of skin was surgically removed, in numerous rectangular patches, from my torso, leaving capillaries and nerve endings exposed. The layer of skin was then stretched into a diamond-patterned mesh and used to cover the exposed muscle tissue on my arms and the full length of both of my legs. The mesh provided a "seed layer" so that new skin could grow.

By the time the grafts had taken and new skin had grown in its place, my muscles had atrophied to where I could ring my thumb and middle finger around my calves. Then I began the painful and frustrating procedure of learning to walk all over again. I stayed in the hospital for more than eight months. Fortunately, I was not badly disfigured by the injuries.

As my body healed, I slowly reconciled myself to the fact that my will to live had overruled death. *My Guardian Angel had saved me for some undisclosed purpose of its own.* I had not been defeated but neither had I completed the blood-right initiation that I had imagined when I joined the army. Rather, my warrior spirit seemed to slip into a shadow zone somewhere between victory over death and defeat. The only thing that was certain was that even though I had confronted death and had the scars to prove it, my initiation was incomplete.

That realization had a lot to do with the fact that I refused the offer of a medical discharge and decided to complete the two years remaining on my military service contract. Perhaps I could even return to the battlefield. The warrior still belonged to the domain of the military, and I did not intend to give up my initiation so easily. For all its faults, the military provided the paternalistic nurturing essential to the warrior—a nurturing that was as deep as the ancient tribal warrior cults on which it was based. I had nearly given up my life to the warlords, and I owed them nothing more. But they owed me. Without the completion of my initiation—in whatever form it might now take—I felt as thought there could be no place for me in civilian society.

I was reassigned to the Department of Tactics at Fort Rucker, Alabama and promoted to the rank of Chief Warrant Officer (CWO-2). Though neither my instinct for flying nor my confidence as a pilot was shattered by the crash, it would be several more months before I would recover sufficiently to return to flight status. I became a training officer in the survival school where we taught cadet pilots escape and evasion techniques should they be shot down, and what they might expect in a prisoner of war camp if captured. Though I considered my new assignment a setback, I was still a soldier.

Outwardly, I conformed to the expectations of my superiors in the performance of my duties, to the limits of propriety afforded by the bars on my cap and collar and to the loyalty oath I had sworn to uphold. But I did not feel that I was master of myself. My loyalty to the military forced me to accept the unanticipated delay in achieving the *mastery-over-self* that, to me, was so importantly implied by the warrior's initiation into selfhood.

Inwardly, my failed initiation created mounting conflicts and frustrations. My training as a warrior had evoked a spirit in me that I could not consciously define, but whose presence in me was, nonetheless, intuited and felt. Still, I had not seen its face and did not know its name. I did not *know* the eternal part of myself that transcended death and would define me and guide me to my destiny. That was the true failure of my initiation, and without that knowledge I felt trapped in a relentlessly mundane reality that stretched the limits of my sanity.

I knew the argument that being guided by spirits could, at best, be called a figment of an overactive imagination or, at worse, pathological psychosis. All the time I was growing up, for example, one of my father's most persistent arguments was that *rational free will raises us above the nonsense of our primitive imaginations.* But my father's military experience did not include the confrontation with death in combat. What I knew for certain about myself was that the blood-lust violence of the killer instinct had been awakened in me. Perhaps it was a lingering remnant of our primordial past when hunters needed to kill in order to feed the tribe—prey and predator locked in a dance-of-death that awakened in our ancestors a transcendent spirit. Or, perhaps it was a remnant of some primordial hunter-warrior who first raised a weapon to defend himself and his tribe against another human being. In either case, in the darkest corridors of my being, the blood-lust still possessed me and could not be easily dismissed as a "figment of my imagination."

I felt it as a hunger, an urge that boiled up from deep inside: a rage that could be easily provoked and not so easily repressed. Even though I knew that those who had killed were tormented by nightmares, I still longed for the taste of blood, and it was that un-punishable license to kill that I missed most about combat. The god of death, whom the

Greeks called *Thanatos,* had been awakened in me, and my failure to confront and triumph over him kept me in his grip. Though my rational free will helped to contain those urges, the rational view of reality did nothing to explain my desire to kill. In my dreams the urge rose-up to challenge my sense of rational self-mastery.

Having returned to civil society meant keeping the primordial killer instinct contained by cultivating a self-image convinced of its own self-mastery. It was a clever self-deception. Still, it described the ordinary way I went about my duties and seemed to describe the way others who had returned from Vietnam went about their duties as well. Most of the men with whom I worked had faced death in combat and, it seemed to me, self-mastery should have been evident in their personalities. But I sensed that it was not. Were they not successfully initiated? Had they met the blood-right requirement for initiation only to find that their power of self-mastery was not acknowledged by their comrades or by the culture? Most of them just wanted to complete their tour of duty and go home, and they seemed to know that the appearance of normalcy— not self-mastery—was the prerequisite for being accepted back into American society. For when Vietnam vets returned from the field of battle, neither the military nor the civilian population acknowledged or helped them celebrate their initiation into selfhood.

That had not been true of WWII, when both soldiers and civilians together celebrated the victory over fascism. The civilian population had followed the conflict with great interest. They, too, had made great sacrifices—the purchase of war bonds, the rationing of vital supplies and working in the factories—to insure our success. After the war, they recognized the individual warrior's trauma of having confronted death on the battlefield for them, and they were grateful and empathetic. The civilian population helped the warriors transform the warrior spirit that had led the march to victory into the kind of energy and passion that rebuilt the post-war society and economy.

But during the Vietnam War, and perhaps because of it, the economy was already strong. The civilian population, though they followed the war on television and were passionately provoked by its political implications, remained distant from the conflict and insensitive to the warrior's individual trauma and pain. The military that had evoked the killer instinct in the inducted recruit did not help either, because it, too, was part of a national consciousness that subverted the individual's sense of self-mastery and replaced it with a façade of normalcy. Thus, the returning Vietnam veteran was not expected to achieve mastery over the warrior spirit and transform its energy and passion toward productive ends. He was only expected to generate the same mask of civility worn by the average citizen so that he could fit back into society. Yet Thanatos festered deep within him. How long would it take for sanity to snap?

Already there were emerging horror-stories of returning veterans who were released directly back into society from the war zone. How could they not have carried the war with them? No longer able to support the burden of the blood on their hands or to contain their inner conflict, many young veterans committed suicide. Others inflicted their revenge on a society that invoked the warrior to serve its political ambitions, but then abandoned him. Either way, the god of death won the battle for the warrior's soul.

In contrast, there was a sense of self-mastery in the older, more seasoned officers and NCOs—the military professionals. It was evident in the way they carried themselves and in the way they spoke. But they had made career commitments before the Vietnam War and their careers would continue after the war was over. War was what they did. Their military professionalism gave them the edge in containing the passions of the warrior, but containment only existed within the context of their commitment to the paternalism of the military establishment. They sacrificed the freedom of their individuality for the regimented life that helped them contain the passions of the warrior. So in that, too, perhaps self-mastery was only an illusion.

The time came for me to make a choice between a military career and returning to civilian life. My commanding officer in Vietnam, Capt. Boyer, had forwarded a recommendation that I be offered the opportunity to attend officers' training school and receive a commission. I agreed to take it on the condition that the military would send me for a tour in Germany. *No, you will be returning directly to Vietnam,* was the military's response. My license to kill would be reinstated. Despite my conflicting emotions about returning to combat, it would be an opportunity to complete the warrior's blood-right initiation into manhood and, therefore, it was an enticing offer.

I gave it some serious consideration. Finally, however, I decided that while a profession in the military would help me contain the passions of the warrior, the price I would have to pay would be the subversion of my individuality. Even though I felt that a discharge would cast me out alone and without support, as had been the case with so many other veterans, I rejected the idea of a military career and began to consider reintegrating, as best I could, back into civilian society. That's when the rebellious streak that I had harbored throughout my adolescence reared its head once more, and I began to rebel against the paternalism of the military.

☆ ☆ ☆

When John, the fourth member of our foursome from flight school, was assigned to Fort Rucker, I acquired an ally in my rebellion. I had not seen John since we had celebrated our graduation together, more than a year before. He had spent two months training with the new *Cobra* gunship before going to Vietnam. During that assignment, he had married his longtime sweetheart, Christine, and they now had a baby boy.

John had proved himself both an exceptional pilot and exceptionally lucky. From what he told me of his tour in Vietnam, I could imagine that John wielded his Cobra gunship as his steed of choice, as easily as a medieval knight on a Clydesdale, and aimed with skill and accuracy, like the knight's lance, the long black fingers of his mini-gun and his side-mounted rocket-pods to bring down his adversary. He came through a year in the war without getting shot down and without a physical scratch. To be sure there were psychological scars, we all carried psychological scars from our combat experience, but he also seemed to be able to contain them. John and I renewed our friendship from flight school with great affection.

He was much more self-assured than me, carrying himself with that same confidence that he had displayed during training which, I assumed, came from having spent a lifetime as part of the military establishment. But, as I got to know his wife Christine, I was certain that she, too, played a major role in the equation that kept John grounded and able to contain the energy and passion of the warrior.

Christine was a strong woman. I did not know how or even if John unburdened the deepest conflicts of his soul, but it seemed to me that she would not be shaken by whatever tribulation he laid on her. She could nurture him with a solidly grounded Earth-Mother spirit. Love—the Greek god *Eros*—was the powerful counterpoint to the hold that the god of death, Thanatos, had over the warrior. It was evident that John and Christine were in love. When they were assigned to Fort Rucker, they moved into a small house off base and established a fairly normal family life away from the rigors of military conformity.

Though John and I both harbored some contempt for the sanctimonious paternalism of the military establishment, we remained loyal to it. Christine provided the counterpoint—the anti-military arguments in our conversations. She was an intelligent and independent woman in the vanguard of the changes in social attitudes that were beginning to emerge in American society. While John was at war, she completed her degree in Political Science, concentrating with particular interest on the policy trends that led the United States to post-WWII military adventurism. Thus, as both an army wife and a serious and knowledgeable critic of the military, Christine straddled two worlds. She attended teas given by the wife of John's commanding officer. But she was also sympathetic to many of the ideas of the hippy movement that had proceeded from the "Summer of Love" and spread across the country while we were being soldiers, though she never referred to herself as a hippy. She was also a vocal advocate for the liberation and empowerment of women, a movement that was still in its early stages. As a modern woman, she was *not* impressed with the chauvinistic bravado of military men who displayed too much of the ostentatious plumage of their inflated egos, and she was not afraid to say so. I understood and sympathized with Christine's perspective. For not having completed my initiation and having rejected the idea of a military career, I did not feel that I would ever become one of them.

That did not matter to John. To him, we were brothers bound by the warrior spirit. We had survived the war and returned to our home base with enough of our wits left to challenge the military authority that, paradoxically, inspired our loyalty with its institutionalized dedication to the warrior and incited our rebellion with its insidious contempt for the strength and individuality of our manhood. Neither of us rebelled to the point of insubordination, but we stretched the limits of military propriety, like the evening we attended a formal reception and dinner at the officer's club and, afterwards, stripped naked for a plunge in the officer's club swimming pool. The lights from the ballroom shone above the pool patio while Christine stood in the shadows, laughing and holding the decorated jackets of our dress blue uniforms.

Emboldened by my friendship with John and Christine, I stretched those limits even further by openly criticizing government policy in free-for-all bull sessions with my colleagues at the office of in the Department of Tactics where I had to report daily in a crisply starched uniform and spit-shined boots. John was assigned to a different division within the same department. He was a gunship training IP, teaching weaponry and tactics to new gunship pilots. During off-duty hours, John spent most of his time with his baby son and with Christine, who was pregnant again. He had a "short-timer's" attitude and ignored, as much as he could get away with, the rigid protocols and procedures of the military establishment. John and Christine incorporated me into their family life. After duty hours, their house became a second home that drew me away from my obsession with the warrior, and I began to take the military and myself a little less seriously.

At their home, we shared long evenings of fondue dinners, bottles of wine and hours of intellectual discussions. These conversations were often stimulated by Christine's interest in and knowledge of government policy issues, which enabled her to criticize the Vietnam War from a well-informed, civilian point of view. But it was a subject that she approached cautiously because John and I were still sensitive to the attitude of the warrior.

She might, for example, begin casually with the news of the day. Stirring the fondue, she would say with calculated casualness, "Did you hear about the antiwar protesters at Harvard taking over the administration building on campus?" Then she turned to me and said, "Oh, would you mind cutting the bread?" John would take that as his cue to duck out and check on the baby, knowing better than to get ambushed by one of Christine's arguments unsympathetic to American militarism.

"Do you think that there is something wrong with that?" I might reply, trying to get a feeling for what she was getting at but, in fact, stumbling head first into the trap.

"All I'm saying is that I agree that someone needs to stand up and protest this war, and the Harvard students are doing what they think is right," she'd reply, feeding the conversation and drawing me in.

From my point of view, it was a complex issue. Regardless of the civilian arguments for and against the war in Vietnam, war is what warriors do.

After putting the baby to bed, John made a picnic, spreading a small tablecloth on the living room floor and surrounding it with pillows. Candles lit the room, providing additional light to the lingering dusk that filtered in through the open windows on a warm spring evening. We carried the fondue, the bread, a salad and two bottles of wine to the living room. There were long forks for dipping the bread in the tasty, gooey, cheese fondue mixture, small plates, bowls for the salad and wine glasses set on the tablecloth. A blue Sterno flame danced beneath the fondue pot, keeping the cheese mixture warm.

Using the same argument that my father would have used, I said, "What is so wrong with the idea of containing communist aggression?" But I really did not have the conviction to defend the so-called "domino theory."

"The Vietnamese just want their country back," she countered and continued with a well-informed dissertation on US government policy failures toward Vietnam from the Truman to the Johnson administrations.

She argued that America was showing signs of the arrogance of power that had weakened and destroyed great nations in the past, openly advancing her argument from Senator J. William Fulbright's 1966 book of the same name. "American imperialism in the guise of justifiable military aggression," she emphasized, "is really not essential to the defense of the nation. It's being excused as necessary to counter communism, but they're really just fighting fire with fire," she continued, implying that taking sides in a foreign civil war was either a faulty strategy or a calculated political deception with undisclosed ulterior motives.

Christine was on a roll. She continued with a criticism of the three-part relationship between the military, industry and the government, arguing that politicians mounted the ideological defense of the more

pragmatic objectives of the military-industrial complex. "They consti-
tute," she said, "a cadre of military, industrial, academic and political
leaders who probably consider themselves *super-patriots.*"

I asked her what she meant by that term.

"Well," she replied, "they probably believe that *they* are responsible for maintaining America's superpower status as the leader of the
Western world against communism. But serving the nation is just a
façade. They are really just arrogant authoritarians who want to control the domestic civilian population and extend American hegemony
abroad for reasons that serve mostly their own economic interests."
She ended with a little giggle of contempt reserved for those who are
smart enough to unmask the real culprits.

Pausing just long enough to let that thought sink in, Christine gin-
gerly pinched a piece of bread, speared it with the fork and dipped
it into the gooey fondue mixture. Then she continued with her argument. "President Eisenhower warned us of the increasing power of the
military-industrial complex. That axis of military and economic power is
now fueling military adventurism in Latin America and Southeast Asia.
And for what?" She answered her own question. "For the defense of
abstractly defined American national interests? The ideological arguments defending those interests are self-righteous and archaically
puritanical."

When I asked her what *should* oppose those objectives, she quickly
added that the nation should be able to rise above such hypocrisy and
be more self-critical and humanistic. "For example, defending and
spreading democracy," she argued, "is an ideological argument. The
real goals have to do with the acquisition of resources and profits by
American corporations that use the military to expand capitalist markets.
The corporations want to exploit the natural resources of the country,
give the Vietnamese peasants work in factories producing cheap goods
for America's consumer market and earn money to buy the kinds of
products from us that they never really needed and can't really afford
to buy. American militarism is subordinate to economic hegemony, and
the concentration of political power is essential to achieving that goal."

Christine sited the Gulf of Tonkin Resolution that gave the president,
not the congress, control over the war-making power of the government and that, she said, upset the checks and balances that were built

into the Constitution, tilting power dangerously in favor of the executive branch.

Congress had to make the effort to restore the balance, but it was really up to the American people to decide which aspect of the American character would dominate—those who represented the American character as an arrogance of power, or the side of the American character that was self-critical and humane.

"It is that self-critical aspect," Christine insisted, "that is the primary motivation not just for the actions of the Harvard students, but for all the war protesters."

I did not have Christine's understanding of government policy, and perhaps she was right. But, while I had my own criticisms of the military, and they were complex, I was still part of that establishment. I became defensive when civilians criticized the military.

"The world is still a dangerous place, Chris. US military strength is essential to containing threats to our freedom, and a military that doesn't fight wars becomes weak. Maybe that means that one of the primary purposes of the Vietnam War is to preserve a strong military, developing new weapons and new tactics. Maintaining a strong military," I said, "is based on more than just the variables of foreign policy, whether that policy defends the objectives of economic growth or ideological hegemony."

While I was only beginning to formulate the concept in my own mind, what I also wanted to say was that the self-mastery implied in the initiation of the warrior was an important element in the perpetuation of a society where individuals first took charge of their own destinies and then shaped their collective destiny in the forum of democracy.

But what I actually said was far less eloquent. "Militarism is part of our psychological makeup and insinuates a wide range of complex, psychological motives in American males that make us want to break away from 'mom and apple pie,' bond with our fellow warriors and confront death in foreign lands. It's an integral part of American male psychology."

John got up to clear the dishes. "Hey, mom, did you bake an apple pie?"

We all laughed.

In one sense, I had to concede that Christine was right. The Vietnam War created a national conflict because it stood at a transformative moment in the on-going evolution of the American identity. In Vietnam, the controversy revolved around the question of whether the warrior was being asked to die to preserve democracy—clearly the case in WWII—or being instructed to kill to preserve the American power structure and its interests around the world. That was the question that I had struggled with in Vietnam. It was the argument that fired the protests, and they were such passionate protests that they caused anti-war activists, the government and the civilian population to abandon the warrior. The possibility that the warrior spirit could be transformed to serve society in positive ways was simply ignored or forgotten, and society did not help the warrior to affect that transformation.

Rather, I felt that a civilian movement led by effete intellectuals, who seemed to consider the initiation of a caste of warriors anachronistic, was defiling the warrior's initiation into selfhood. The returning soldier was expected to act as though his confrontation with death, the death he inflicted on the battlefield and the blood on his hands were events in his life to simply be set aside. By turning against the warrior, anti-war and anti-military activists denied him confirmation, denied him transformation, denied him re-integration and demanded that his warrior spirit remain buried in his unconscious. But such self-denial could only lead to the insidious perversion of the personality. By burying the warrior in the unconscious, the war continued as an unresolved conflict between a spirit dominated by Thanatos and the rational behaviors of the ego that fulfilled the expectations of civil society. The soul was the battleground that lay between the spirit and the ego.

Thus denied and ignored, the returning warrior was unconfirmed in his inner power to master his own destiny. Rather than stand tall as an icon of the self-directed citizen of American democracy, the Vietnam veteran was worn-out by his internal struggle, rejected as a no longer relevant tool of the warlords of the patriarchy and marginalized by "civil" society.

Though it had been more than a year since I had left the battlefield, I was still struggling with my unresolved, internal conflict. I felt, more than ever, the need for an intimate confirmation of the strength of my warrior spirit so that I could transform its energies. While I found comfort in being included in John's and Christine's home life, I did not find that confirmation with them. Neither did I find consolation with my own family. They were all far away and involved in the pursuits of their own lives.

In order to contain the shadowy spirit that festered in the dark corridors of my unconscious and took shape in my dreams, I began to channel my energy toward strengthening my rational intellect. I read the works of different philosophers, but I was particularly enamored with Frederich Nietzsche and began reading nearly all of his works. I also made up my mind to complete my college education. There were no architecture courses offered by Troy State, the small, Liberal Arts University that operated a branch at Fort Rucker. Instead I studied mathematics, with a double minor in history and art, and graduated with honors. The result was that my personality was pulled between two extremes—the still frustrated, feeling-toned passions of the warrior spirit and the outwardly cool egotism of a willful, rational intellect. My soul, which lay between those extremes, was being crushed. That was when I met Pat.

☆ ☆ ☆

Like my mother, Pat was an Alabamian. She was a civilian employee of the army who worked at one of Fort Rucker's three airfields. We met soon after I returned to flight status. I went to the airfield to check out an aircraft to meet my monthly flight requirement, maintain my proficiency and log as much flight time as I could before being discharged. Pat took care of the paperwork, so I had to check in with her before taking the aircraft and check out with her when I returned. She always had a smile for me and she was kind. Though she was not a great beauty, I found in her an Earth Mother attractiveness that promised to be nurturing. I made it a point to log my flight time from the airfield to which she was assigned. We saw each other frequently, and it was not long before we began dating.

Indeed, it was probably that nurturing quality in Pat that gave her the power to quell my intellectualism and redirect my passions. Over a long dinner at a local restaurant, she listened attentively while I constructed an intellectual argument about whatever topic was on my mind at the moment. Then she would smile, reach across the table and stroke my arm. Her touch, like a mild electric shock, interrupted my logic. I stumbled. We laughed. She wasn't mocking me. I knew that she understood what I was saying, but she was not interested in countering my argument, as Christine would have done. Pat had a way of making me see that all my intellectual babble was cerebral and defensive. What she was interested in was not what I thought but what I felt.

It was that capacity to address and redirect my feelings that made our relationship special. Pat, a divorcee without children, was several years older than me. She had been married to a military man and had already been through the painful experience of learning to cultivate the patience required within an intimate relationship with a wounded warrior. She understood the warrior spirit.

One stormy night, after dinner and a few drinks, we went to a local movie theater to see *Thunder Road*, a classic, black-and-white Robert Mitchum film-noire of car chases and random violence. The storm made the electricity flicker, interrupting the film several times. We laughed it off. Then, the film broke. Waiting for the projectionist to repair the film, I grew irritated. Then, irritation grew to frustration and frustration built toward rage. Outside thunder cracked and the lights in the theater flickered on and off, like night flashes on the battlefield. Suddenly, I had a flashback of Camp Evans under rocket attack. Pat knew instinctively what to say and what to do to calm the rekindled fire of combat. We left the theater and spent the rest of the evening in her home.

We soon agreed that we were both more comfortable in the privacy of her home than in public places. Rather than go out on dates, we spent leisurely evenings in domestic bliss. As we got to know each other, she expressed a warmth and tenderness toward me to which I was not accustomed. It helped me to recover some of the tenderness that had long been closed off, and I opened myself to her touch—a touch I had not felt from a woman since my mother's death. Pat made me the same kinds of home-cooked meals that my mother had made—southern fried chicken, mashed potatoes with gravy, fresh-cut green beans, warm biscuits with honey-butter and pineapple upside-down cake for dessert. She understood, instinctively, my simplest needs. More important, she was not disturbed by the scaring of my body, which was a very sensitive issue with me.

In the peacefulness of her home, a comfortable distance—physically and psychologically—from the military, we listened to music while she caressed and kissed my wounded body with affection. My passions sank into my loins. We fell on the bed, and she kissed the fire that raged within me with cool lips. I welcomed the embrace that soothed my inner rage and buried my shaft inside her with a gentle thrust and peri-thrust that made her shiver with delight. She held me tight and closed her eyes to love.

I did not retreat from the mutual joy of our orgasm, but neither did I allow it to seduce me into a commitment that I did not want to make. I was much too naïve about women to be able to read the subtle signs, and I really did not know if a commitment is what she ultimately wanted. I had to beg that her gifts did not ask too much in return. When her body surged, she squeezed the muscles of my neck and shoulders in response and seemed to lose herself in that moment of ecstasy. I found my own release but could not surrender all. Sometimes I even imagined that I awoke in her the memory of another that she held in her dreams, but not me. I still felt like an uninitiated warrior. I was an incomplete person, and she could not complete me.

With Pat, I realized that what was missing from the decade of my adolescence was that undefined, ethereal part of my being called the soul. It was a missed step on my march toward modern manhood. What I had gotten instead was my father's sensible and pragmatic worldview, which had left me little room for emotional expression. As a result, the dreams and visions of my youth had never crossed the threshold of erotic engagement with the world to give meaning to my endeavors—not with my friends and relationships in high school, not with my mentor-apprentice relationship with Al Ramp and not with my relationship with Carl. When the military offered me the warrior's lance, I sprang too eagerly to grasp it.

I suppose the trauma of my mother's death had been mostly responsible for the burying of my feelings. A mother's touch might have stimulated my soul, smoothed the roughness of my adolescent ego, softened the edges of my personality and awakened my Eros spirit to oppose the god of death. Now, even though Pat gratified my body and stirred a new awareness deep down in my soul, she did not awaken the mystery of the Eros spirit that lay buried beneath the warrior. How bitter it was to recall my loss and reflect on what might have been. The damage was already done, yet I was determined to rescue my soul from the shadows.

With that new determination, I realized that Pat, who embraced me as a gentle lover, and John and Christine, who shared their family life with me, had been placed in my path by Fate and my neglected soul began to awaken. It would no longer be treated with contempt, and I began to explore, in the metaphor of poetry, the mystery of my inner being.

> *What form or shade is this*
> *That dwells in me,*
> *And swells me with eternal song?*

I spoke directly of my soul as the unknown power of Eros dwelling within me.

> *Is there no face to give you form?*
> *Why do my senses dull when you come near?*
> *When they should sparkle with excitement,*
> *Not with fear.*

My mysterious soul rose up as a soft, feminine guide within me.

> *Could you be my Beatrice?*
> *Could all this love manifest*
> *In one magnificent human form?*
> *Are you here to lead me to an unknown paradise?*

At other times, my soul was stirred by my desire for an intimate friendship, and Mike's face would appear to repair all my fragmented relationships.

> *Perhaps then you are a deeper, more eternal thing,*
> *The bond of two who long for love*
> *That's greater than the earthly stride.*

Then, my fantasies faded, and I was once more alone.

> *Perhaps then, soul, Love of my eternity,*
> *You are all these things in me.*

From John, I learned that Mike had also survived Vietnam. He was assigned to Fort Wolters as a flight instructor. I thought of him often and wondered how his gentle sensitivities had coped with his experience in Vietnam, but I never saw him again.

Mike's soul was too gentle to contain, for very long, the inner conflict between the god of death and the expectations of a civil society. On a dark, rainy night, three years after being discharged from the army and lubricated with alcohol, the god of death took hold of Mike and drove him, at seventy miles an hour, into a tree.

☆ ☆ ☆

While John and Christine and I remained close during the remainder of our tour at Fort Rucker, John began to focus on his ambition to become an airline pilot. He was accepted at a civilian flight school where he would continue his education and training after his service obligation was complete.

My dream was to escape not only the military but from a society where rigid controls over the expressions of the personality inhibited me from finding a resolution to my inner conflict between the intimidations of Thanatos and all the unfulfilled promise of Eros. Anticipating the fulfillment of that dream, as my military obligation neared completion I wandered further away from the military establishment and spent long weekend passes in New Orleans, the sensual jewel of the south and a five-hour drive from Fort Rucker.

☆ ☆ ☆

The city pulsated with the rhythmic improvisations of jazz, inviting improvisations on the theme of life. It was a mecca for discomforted Southern misfits, much as Greenwich Village was a mecca in the northeast. Both the Village and the Big Easy continued to reverberate the chord struck on the streets of San Francisco's Haight-Ashbury during the Summer of Love that initiated the hippy movement several years before. When I went to New Orleans, I tried to integrate myself into that ambiance, but the contrast was too sharp. My short-cropped hair, my ill-fitting civilian clothes from the PX and my own feeling that I could not disguise the discipline of self-vigilance engrained in me as a young army officer, all kept me on the sidelines—an observer to a bizarre sideshow of life.

Each time I went to New Orleans, there seemed to be some local festival in progress, and an atmosphere of gaiety and abandon prevailed. Strands of jazz—from a coronet, a keyboard, a trombone and a base—floated out of every bar door and moved in twisting arabesques down the street, inspiring drunken tourists to attempt an uncoordinated dance-step, as they laughed and stumbled toward their hotels. I watched quietly from the sidelines and stayed up late, long after the conventioneers had passed out in their hotel rooms and the streets had become the background for the nightshift of characters whose personal dramas unfolded in the midnight shadows. There I had my first encounter with hippies.

I did not remember the months leading up to the *Summer of Love,* for they took place during the year I was inducted into the army and was learning to fly helicopters. While hippies were making love, I was preparing to make war. The idealistic sentiments of the "love generation" escaped me, for I was thoroughly enmeshed in meeting the expectations of the warlords of the patriarchy. All those things that had to do with the liberation of the soul—the music and the dancing, the freedom of expression and the carefree abandon, the sharing and the innocence—were not part of my reality.

Then, it seemed, at some undefined moment following the summer of '67, the idealistic foundations of the hippy movement pivoted almost imperceptibly on a pillar of marijuana smoke, a tab of LSD, a line of cocaine. The real idealists faded into the background, setting up communes in Kentucky and Oregon or joining the Buddhists, the Hari-Krishnas or other cult movements. What was left on the streets was a rag-tag band of young people mostly strung-out on drugs and sequestered together in the shadows of the night. Those were the hippies that I met in New Orleans.

With their backpacks and their long, stringy hair, they hung-out on the streets. There were pimply teenagers who should have still been in high school, college students and college drop-outs, and young people who had joined the movement hoping for the opportunity to forge their own life's adventure, as I had forged mine in the military. They smoked dope openly but discretely, watching for cops. I had never used drugs, not even in Vietnam, though now I was tempted to try marijuana. The drug seemed, from my point of view, to be important in developing a counterculture attitude—something that altered perceptions, helped them to loosen-up and escape from the rigid expectations that imposed the unspoken controls of society on the individual. I watched from the sidelines with mixed emotions: contempt cultivated by the cool self-vigilance of a young army officer, and envy for a lifestyle that I also wanted but did not feel that I had the freedom to explore.

They were not the only characters populating the late night streets of New Orleans. Flamboyant pimps in slick polyester suits drove shiny cars and bullied their whores who stood on street corners in spiked high heels, fishnet stockings, mini-skirts and bulging blouses, smiling at passers by. When they smiled at me, my naïve character shied away from the darker-side of Eros, in whom intimacy was corrupted by money. I turned my eyes to the ground and walked on in silence.

Adolescent runaways from conservative Southern towns hung out in pinball parlors waiting for *johns* to buy their pussies and their cocks. I wondered if they were driven by desperation to escape a home-life of violence or boredom and that, now, selling their young bodies was a foregone conclusion of the rough economics of street life. Or did they derive some ephemeral pleasure from illicit sex—from a Dionysian spirit reveling in its own excesses?

Faggots cruised the streets and ducked in and out of gay bars. When they eyed me with a look that said, *come here, army boy, and let me show you what my gun can do,* I smiled back at them, teasing the Eros spirit that blew like an unconscious wind through their souls, looking openly for the love whose name in America still could not be spoken. And there were transvestites who shattered the stillness of the night with hysterical shrieks—a travesty of the feminine within, crying out of the masculine psyche in a neurotic possession of the personality.

One night, *Tinkerbelle* caught my eye as he/she staggered across the street in a drunken stupor, trailing yards of tacky silk scarf and stumbling in faded high heels after a *trick*. I laughed out loud, and my laughter broke through the transparent barrier that kept me on the outside of that bizarre world, looking in. I sipped my beer and, in an unaccustomed mood of conviviality, struck up a conversation with a man who sat next to me at the bar. Thus, I opened, just a crack, the doorway into a strange and fascinating reality that seemed to be stumbling through time out of control, filled with both the ecstasies and torments of the soul. Yet, paradoxically, to me it seemed more fully alive than the normalcy it had left behind.

Stirred by such provocations, my passions were driven into the helmet of my phallic shaft, where they begged for release, but I found no comfort from the characters of the street. Still, the fishnet stockings on the smooth legs of bubble-gum chewing whores, the tight, round asses and smooth baskets of desperate adolescent boys, the come-hither look of faggots and the shrillness of Tinkerbelle all shocked my senses into awakening. I returned to my hotel room and released, in lonely, frustrated, fantasy-fueled strokes, the tension that was building in my soul.

Beneath my hardened exterior, my erotic vitality was slowly recovering, lifting me above the disappointments of my youth, raising me up out of the ashes of my frustrated initiation and promising me liberation. My erotic vitality held the promised gift of new life that whispered soft seductions, and it no longer seemed so frightening. I sensed that therein lay the power with which I could complete my initiation. That gave me a new goal in life that could not be restrained by either the military or the expectations and demands of civilian society. I needed to liberate the Eros spirit in my soul and to explore its full potential. In watching from a distance, I sensed that there were those among the characters of the night who explored the soul's inner mysteries, and it was comforting to know that I would not be alone.

The remainder of my military obligation passed swiftly, and I was determined to make a clean-break from the system that applied so much pressure to control my destiny. I decided to go to Europe. The cheap airfares of the early seventies had opened the portal to Europe for hundreds of thousands of young Americans. Some were escaping from the military draft. Others, like me, were pursuing relief from a society that was unsympathetic to the cry of anguish from a tormented, youthful soul. I held on to a hope that, in seeking the same thing, our quests would merge. We could learn from each other how to transform ourselves, and together we would learn to rejoin American society as positive contributors to the transformation of our collective future.

CHAPTER SEVEN:

Munich

I was honorably discharged from the army in June of 1970, graduated from college with a Bachelor's degree in mathematics in August and went home. I was twenty-four years old.

My father and his second wife still lived in Oak Park. They had bought a larger house where they lived with a hybrid-family consisting of her two children and my youngest brother who was about to enter college. My aunt and uncle in California were still raising my baby sisters. My older sister, Pat, was married and had a child. My brother, Bill, who was exempt from the draft because of a childhood injury, was living in Oak Park with his fiancé and her young daughter from an earlier marriage.

Though I stayed in my father's house, it was evident to me that I no longer fit into that home and family life. During my three and a half years in the military, they had all moved on with their lives within parameters that, I suppose, they considered normal. I was locked out of their definition of normalcy by experiences that I still could not explain to myself, much less to them. Those family attachments had been left behind, and I was beginning to realize just how much I was on my own. Perhaps they expected that I would, somehow, squeeze myself back into the comfortable parameters that defined their lives. Or perhaps, preoccupied with their own affairs, they really didn't care what I did.

Though I was determined to pursue my plan to go to Europe—in some way a follow-up on the trip I had planned to take with Carl in 1966—I had also decided that I wanted to finish my degree in architecture.

Toward that end, in early September, I visited several universities in the Midwest, hoping to enroll for the winter semester, but I was not made to feel welcome. My old school, the University of Illinois at Urbana, told me that they had reorganized the department and now offered a five-year Master's degree program in architecture. The course requirements had changed, and they would not accept most of the credits from the architecture courses that I had taken six years earlier, nor would they recognize my degree in mathematics. They were not impressed that I was a decorated and honorably discharged army officer who had served in the Vietnam War. Just what the hell did they want from me? They smiled and said they would gladly re-enroll me in a five-year undergraduate program and accept the money from my GI Bill.

From each school that I visited, I received the same cold reception, the same sense that I was just not welcomed back into the American community, the same sense that the opportunity to pursue my goals was somehow tainted by my involvement in the war. It was depressing to feel the sting of rejection and misunderstanding that greeted all Vietnam veterans who were trying to re-integrate into American society—the same rejection that drove so many veterans away from their homes and families and onto the streets. I put my university plans on hold, bought an Icelandic Airline ticket from New York to Luxembourg and boarded a bus to New York, the Big Apple. There was enough money in my savings account to buy the airline ticket, a three-month Eurail Pass, pocket money for a three-month grand tour of Europe and money for when I returned.

I had an older cousin living in New York who worked for Radio Free Europe and was able to put me up for a couple of days while I visited the city and waited for my flight. That turned out to be fortuitous. We did not know each other well, so it was an opportunity to get reacquainted. My cousin gave me the name of her friend, Dave, who also worked for R.F.E. in their offices in Munich, Germany. She assured me that, should I decide to go to Munich, Dave would probably put me up for a few days. I had no plan, no itinerary. I just wanted to leave the country and have the opportunity to look at the United States from a different perspective.

☆ ☆ ☆

On the flight to Luxembourg I met Paul, a sixteen year-old American boy who was traveling alone to visit his older brother stationed with the army in Munich. I did not tell him about my experience in the war. Instead, I listened with interest to Paul's story.

The previous summer, he had visited Munich with his parents then stayed on after his parents returned to the United States. Through some friends of his brother, Paul learned about an agency in Munich that arranged to deliver newly purchased, German-made automobiles to customers in the Middle East. The agency recruited young travelers in pairs to transport the vehicles. They were given money for their travel expenses and paid for the service. Paul had the opportunity to drive a newly purchased Mercedes-Benz from Munich to Kabul, Afghanistan. From Kabul, Paul had traveled over the Hindu Kush, through the tribal lands of Pakistan and on to Kathmandu, Nepal. The adventure helped him to set a career goal, and Paul decided that he wanted to be a cartographer.

Paul was only fifteen years old when he made that journey, and he introduced me to what I considered a refreshing, new permissiveness in the way he had been raised of which I could easily be envious. As I listened to his adventure, and how he had manipulated his high school education to fit the itinerary of his desires, I felt that this American youth, only a few years younger than me, had already acquired a world-liness that was far beyond his years. I wondered if Paul was indicative of a newly emerging generation of world-wise, sophisticated travelers who had the intelligence and sensitivity to make valuable comparisons between American culture and the cultures in which they traveled. He made me feel as though I was the naïve one. My only experience in a foreign country was under the close supervision of the military and closed to an understanding of Vietnamese culture. For the first time, I was setting out on an adventure to actively seek knowledge of other cultures, and Paul was already far ahead of me.

Though I was alone on this trip to Europe and feeling nakedly vulnerable, It was an opportunity to begin anew and to develop the instincts for adaptability that had laid dormant most of my life and which stood in stark contrast to the disciplined conformity I had learned in the army. Paul's adventure inspired me toward the realization of my new freedom and encouraged the belief that I was going to meet fellow travelers along the way. I landed in Europe filled with the promise of a new awakening.

Together, Paul and I hitchhiked to Munich. I had never hitchhiked before, and I let him take the lead.

It was late September, and the *Oktoberfest* was just beginning. Paul went to stay with his brother. I had Dave's address and phone number in my pocket and, just as my cousin had predicted, he was willing to put me up for a few days. Then, at one of the festival events, I met a young Canadian. We decided to travel together through Austria and Switzerland, but it was a short-lived adventure. He was enrolled in a school to study French in Geneva. So, on a lonely country road in Switzerland, we separated. Once more I found myself alone.

Both Paul and the Canadian boy had sparked my desire for a companion of the spirit with whom to share this new adventure. Sharing the adventure is what I had wanted, and what had been frustrated, when I arrived in Vietnam with Mike. In a subtle and almost unconscious way, finding a companion is what I had anticipated from the adventure of coming to Europe alone. But now that I was alone again, the disappointment of that desire left me deeply depressed.

I arrived in Bern, Switzerland with that depression weighing heavily upon me. The weighty feeling stayed with me throughout the day and into the night, while I wandered the streets of the city. I had no plan and did not know which way to turn. Never in my life had I been without some kind of plan to guide me, yet here I was alone and without direction. It was a new experience and a little frightening. My mind flashed from possibility to possibility—one road leading here, another road leading there. It was as if the four gates of the city tempted me to fly on the wind and tore me simultaneously in all four directions. Finally, exhausted from the emotional turmoil of the struggle with myself, I sat down on a dark stairway in the shadows of the lamp-lit city, turned my face to the heavens, emptied my mind and searched for a sign that would lead me out of my depression.

I looked at the silver stars dancing in a cloudless, moonless sky and found the three stars that formed Orion's belt. I remembered from many years before how, when we lived on the farm, my father had pointed out those same three stars and told me the story of Orion. It was one of the few constellations that I could locate and, through the years, I often had looked at those three stars trying, without success, to decipher the enigma, trying to find the form of the great hunter in the sky.

Suddenly, I recognized the star that represented his shoulder. Then, I found Orion's head and knee and Sirius, the loyal *Dog Star* that followed Orion across the heavens. As I stared up at them, each dim star became more brilliant, shining with a spark of familiarity, and the figure began to emerge. For the first time, I formed in my mind's eye the complete outline of Poseidon's luckless son, crossing the dark night sky.

Like the warrior, Orion the hunter knew that intimate dance-of-death between predator and prey. In the silence of the forest, he played the game—the stealth and strategy of the hunt—and felt the excitement of confrontation when the blade-point of his spear drove the spirit of the vanquished animal back into the ethers from which it came. I recalled the story.

Out hunting one day, alone in the forest, the blood-lust overtook Orion, and he had a desire to kill all the creatures of the earth. I knew the feeling. Though the blood-lust had never possessed me so completely, I knew the god of death was still lurking deep inside me. *The gods could not allow the great hunter to act on his desire and petitioned Zeus, who sent a giant scorpion to kill him. However, feeling compassion for his nephew, Zeus placed them both in the night sky, where the constellation Scorpio follows behind Orion for all eternity.*

Visible from Asia, America and Europe, the mythic son of Poseidon was a mysterious presence with whom I felt somehow connected. He always kept me oriented in the cosmos. He centered me in a way that countered my sense of alienation in this new environment.

When my gaze returned once again to the lamp-lit streets and the quaint shuttered buildings of Bern, they no longer looked so foreign. The light on the cobblestones no longer threatened me with harsh, illuminated arrows pointing outward through the four gates of the city. Now each street simply beckoned with a soft, seductive whisper that fell from the lips of the night breeze, "Come. Follow where I lead."

In that moment, I had an epiphany. I realized that the European adventure that awaited me was mine alone. It was to be a quest for my soul—as yet to be discovered—that could not be compromised by others. This realization made me reflect on how passive the quarter-century of my life had been—how dependent, how conditioned, how stripped of the active prerogative by forces in society that pushed and shoved, guiding and controlling my life through high school, university, my job and the military. Only now, in the transition from the military back to civilian life, when I had arrived in Europe without expectations, free from the shackles of my culture and without social burdens and responsibilities, did I become fully responsible for my own life. Before me stretched an open pathway that beckoned in any direction that I would choose. But the choice would come from me alone, filling the barren landscape of my soul with encounters drawn from my imagination, giving shade and texture, light and shadow to that unknown part of myself. I realized that Europe was where I needed to be and that I would not be going home any time soon.

The following morning, I left Bern with a springier step and a new glow in my face.

✰ ✰ ✰

My pathway led me next to Paris, where I was greeted with led-gray skies and an ill-mannered people who made me resolute never to return. There, I met an English youth with whom I traveled on to London. I stayed in the flat that he shared with friends near Nottinghill Gate, but I was anxious to get out of London and explore more of the country.

I spent a total of six weeks in England. It was Europe without the language barrier. Understanding the language and conversing with people helped me begin to understand them, and I became better oriented to what I called the *psychological texture* of Europe. The anxiety I had felt when I was alone in Switzerland helped me realize that my orientation to this foreign environment was just as important as it had been in Vietnam. Like many other veterans, my psyche was still fine-tuned to the requirements of survival, and I sensed that keeping myself together depended on a new orientation to the European mentality.

Several people that I knew in the States had provided me with the addresses of friends and relatives in England. From London, I went up to Oxford where John's younger sister, Anne, was enrolled in school.

Anne, whom I found to be a liberated woman much like her sister-in-law, Christine, seemed, like Paul, to be another one of those worldly-wise, and sophisticated young people who could adapt easily to a new culture. I sensed that she had already embraced a new European-oriented worldview. In the course of my long discussions with Anne, I found an encouraging stimulus that helped me look more closely at myself. For example, when I told her about my disappointing attempt to return to the study of architecture in an American university and how rejected it had made me feel, she said, "So, why don't you apply to Oxford?"

Caught off-guard by her simple solution to overcoming my own passivity and self-pity, I had to ask myself, "Why not?" I was still angry and hurt by those who had summarily dismissed my efforts to reconstitute training toward a professional career, but my conversations with Anne convinced me that I had the intelligence to get into Oxford University and that I should take a more active stance. Since I was already determined to stay in Europe, perhaps even until the end of the war, the idea fulfilled my need to find a plausible excuse. At first, however, I was only amused by the thought of acquiring a significant graduate degree from one of the world's most prestigious universities—a barb to prick the corpulence of the ruling establishment and extract my revenge against the American ruling patriarchy that had tainted the promise of my initiation into selfhood.

Yet, I still retained a pragmatic notion that I could discover a new calling and eventually reintegrate as a positive contributor to American society. I took Anne's suggestion and scheduled interviews with several colleges. I was well received by the Oxford dons who seemed genuinely impressed with my maturity, my experience in the military, the way I presented and expressed myself and with my serious academic objectives.

My academic interests had progressed from architecture through urban planning, and I now stated my objectives as an intention to read for a graduate degree in philosophy. Based on my bachelor degree in mathematics, it was a logical choice. Still, though I had been reading the works of some philosophers and carried one of Nietzsche's books in my backpack, my newly awakened interest in a serious study of philosophy took me a little by surprise. It revealed an academic bent that differed remarkably from the professional training in architecture that had been my fixation since the age of fourteen and which, in so many ways, had been an outgrowth of the expectations of my youth. In contrast to a university education focused on professional training, the black-robed dons of Oxford seemed medieval in their rigorous pursuit of pure knowledge. Studying philosophy under the tutorial system at Oxford provided a perfect environment in which to pursue the intellectual track.

The dons listened to my solicitation without prejudging my motives either for having served in the military or wanting to continue my education. When they asked me why I wanted to study philosophy, I stated my theory that the United States, while preaching individual freedom, was really a society tightly controlled by intangible forces that limited individual expression. Those forces demanded unrelenting conformity with the threat of social ostracism and disenfranchisement if one could not or did not conform. Growing up in the comfort of the white middle class, those entrenched American racial, ethnic, religious and gender prejudices seemed theoretical and distant. But now as a Vietnam veteran, I had felt the sting of ostracism and disenfranchisement myself. I wanted to understand the dynamics of the authority behind those intangible forces.

Expressing that theory was my first attempt to intellectually articulate my feelings about my failed initiation. I wanted to know why the ruling patriarchy seemed so intent on subverting the self-mastery that was a natural outcome of the initiation experience and the right of the warrior who heroically confronted and overcame death. While I talked, the dons seemed to be examining both the passion behind my motives and my capacity to express myself. Finally, they nodded and encouraged me to take the entrance exam.

During that week of interviews and exams, I leapt past the pedantic, judgmental and hypocritical attitudes that I had encountered at universities in the States. The Oxford dons encouraged me to explore the depth and originality of my own thoughts as they had been molded by my life's experiences. That bit of encouragement gave me a new confidence in the power of my own mind. I no longer felt like an impotent appendage of the American patriarchy, where my choices in life were confined by the narrow limits of conformity established by unseen powers. I could leave that old self-image behind.

Assured that the university would notify me of their decision in due course, I returned to London where I stayed with Monty and

Rose—godparents of my best friend from high school. They welcomed me with dignified English hospitality and allowed me to use their home in Mill Hill as a base from which to explore London and apply to several other universities. When my own plans to travel to the south of England coincided with Monty's plan to look at property to buy on the south coast, they invited me along for the trip.

The psychological temper of rural England contrasted with scholarly Oxford and also differed from the focused self-consciousness that kept the frantic pace of urban life in London attuned to a collective rhythm of individual self-determination. The countryside seemed to unfold as a magnificent dreamscape of symbolic and feeling-toned impressions through which Monty steered his classic Mercedes with unconscious ease. In County Kent, fields of freshly cut barley and hay filled the air with the smells of the autumn harvest. The October sun shone through the scattered clouds, making the countryside glow with a bright, fiery light so exquisitely captured in Turner's landscapes. Farmers worked the fields. Women carried baskets to village markets. Children rode bicycles on rut-worn country roads. But among those people, it seemed the existential forms of individuality gave way to more subtle margins of tone and texture so that the scenery and ourselves within it merged into a single, finely wrought tableau. Thus, I was taken in by the powerful feeling of being absorbed into a timeless, magical reality that was characteristic of the landscape of the soul and caused my soul to shine through my ego's outer shell, like an embryo in an egg mysteriously lit from within.

We drove south to Brighton on the English Channel, where we stayed the night. Then, over breakfast, Monty and Rose had a long discussion that weighed the pros and cons of turning west toward Southampton and up to the Salisbury Plain and Stonehenge, or looking at property to the east of Brighton. I was just along for the ride and had securely woven myself into the fabric of their choices.

From my point of view, I was just a mysterious captive of the unconscious essence of rural England and thoroughly absorbed in the wonderful sensation of magic that I had not felt since I was a child. Beneath the luster of modern England, beneath the long historical trail of Norman, Anglo-Saxon and Roman invasions lay the mystical ambience of the Druids of my Celtic ancestors. When Monty had mentioned the possibility of going to Stonehenge, it suddenly brought back a memory of my Aunt Francine's stories of my maternal lineage stretching back through the Moon family line to the Druids. Being absorbed in the timeless, magical reality of rural England connected me to that heritage.

But finally, Monty and Rose decided to go east through Hastings, Dover and Canterbury and then back to London. The sharp contrast between the stillness of the countryside and the noises and distractions of the city again forced me to focus on self-consciousness—to focus on the struggle *not* to allow myself to be absorbed into the chaos of urban surroundings. But I had made the connection with my cultural heritage and to a mystical reality that was not just English but European and more profound than I could possibly have imagined.

The experiences in Oxford and County Kent gave me a feeling for the psychological texture of Europe. Perhaps even more importantly, it gave me a new confidence that I could adapt to this culture, much as Anne and Paul had done. I characterized that texture as being more open to the mystical forces that permeate our lives, mystical forces that were not in opposition to, but in harmony with, the rational view of the world. This experience awakened dormant memories of the Goddess of the Moon in an Illinois cornfield and of the mysterious allure of my Druid ancestors. It reminded me of my encounter with that shadowy messenger that preceded my mother's death and the Angel of Death on board the USS Sanctuary in the South China Sea. Those were earlier mystical encounters in my life that I had accessed through my imagination, intuition and feelings. But they had so contradicted the rational and pragmatic view of reality that was the lesson of my upbringing that, at the time, I repressed them. Now, those earlier encounters with the mystical—with the mysterious essence of life—were confirmed, and I was finally able to open myself to a new and different—a more complete—view of reality.

I interpreted both the magical road trip with Monty and Rose and my encounter with philosophers at Oxford as a direct challenge to the pragmatic, American way of thinking. It awakened me to a new idea that knowledge was not an absolute that dramatically disrobed or casually dismissed the mysteries of life and drained them of their potency. Rather, knowledge had to stand as a counterpoint to those mysteries. Openness to the mystery-of-life tilted the scales on which a life was weighed against empirical certainty; tilted it back in favor of a balance between the two. Sir Isaac Newton, one of the greatest minds of the European Enlightenment, had also been a student of Alchemy and thus had recognized the significance of finding the balance between the empirical certainties of Enlightenment rationalism and that mysterious essence that permeates all life.

It seemed to me that the European psyche was more balanced in that respect, more open to a timeless, magical web of energy that permeated both the individual and the culture. Thus individual self-awareness and self-determination were always tempered by their links to the collective society and to the past. The individual was more harmoniously balanced between a unique individuality and the seamless continuum of the culture of which he or she was a part. I could see that in Monty and Rose, who slipped so effortlessly between the conscious demands of urban life and the mystical, unconscious essence of the countryside.

I was anxious to explore that new energy in myself, yet I remained cautious. As an American, I had inherited the propensity to look toward the future, for we were all cut-off from the past and, thus, without the anchor of a cultural heritage. Though I had begun to feel the essence of my long-lost heritage, I also knew that the energy that I pictured as a *spirit-wind* could easily shift me this way or that, out of control, and throw me into chaos. I had felt that way on the streets of Bern only weeks before. If I opened and attuned myself to a mysterious spirit-wind to steer me through the landscape of the soul, then I would be accepting the idea that self-mastery was not so much a process of self-conscious determination but, rather, acceptance of a spiritual force that comes from within. Now that I was out of the military, I was no longer certain that the warrior spirit guided my destiny, and I would have to become more conscious of all of the spiritual forces in my life.

I wrote my father, explaining as best I could why I felt that I had to stay in Europe. I sent him my unused Eurail Pass and the return portion of my Icelandic Airline ticket, asking him to cash them and send me the money, care of Dave's address. I had decided to return to Munich, where I knew I could find work to support myself through the winter months and await the answers to my applications to British universities.

☆ ☆ ☆

The cold, clear days of December stung my senses with vitality, and I found the people of Munich vibrant and bustling with an urban energy that was contagious. Once more, I was able to stay in Dave's apartment. With his encouragement, I set out to acquire my work papers and a job, for at that time it was easy to get papers as a *guest worker* in Germany.

The holiday festivities were just beginning, and I found a job with an old Munich establishment, the Adolph Käfer Restaurant, that had contracts to cater many of the official Christmas parties in the city. Throughout the month of December, both private companies and departments of the government held lavish holiday banquets for their employees in the art museums, the famous Nymphenburg Palace and in the Antiquarium Hall of the state Residence of the dukes, princes and kings who had ruled Bavaria for 500 years. Thanks to my friend Carl and his parents, I was already familiar with some aspects of German culture that preceded the stain of Nazism. It seemed to me that those festivities linked the Germans who attended them with that long and lustrous cultural heritage. Architectural masterpieces, restored from the damage suffered in World War II, were once again filled with light, music and laughter, awakening the ephemeral ghosts of Ludwig's Munich to parade through the corridors of memory, reviving the timeless, magical cultural reality of the city.

Monks, *Mönche* in German, founded the city a thousand years ago on the banks of the Isar River. Nobles with such illustrious names as Albrecht, Maximilian and Ludwig ruled the city that, at one time, was called the "Athens on the Isar" in reference to Munich's function as a center for culture and art.

In my catering job I only served the wine and washed the dishes, but still I felt as though I had a privileged glimpse into the historic past of German culture. I had taken a year of German language courses before going into the army. My German was not very good but, as I listened to conversations of the people at the banquets, I opened up my feelings and intuition so that my limited understanding was also filtered through my imagination. The totality of words and sensations flooded my mind with vivid images of a long line of German nobility, stretching back into the mythic past of gods and heroes and swords, alchemy and magic. Thus was evoked a phantasmagoric impression of the German soul that, like the peeling of an onion, consisted of layer upon layer of historical strata surrounding an unknowable, unreachable primordial core. That vision of the German soul stimulated my own soul. Like two lovers in the night, the exchange of soul energies broke down the barriers that separated my ego from the soul-space within me. It allowed the spirit-wind to penetrate and influence me in new and subtle ways.

I did not change overnight. But in that foreign environment, where I was free from the influences of social conditioning in America, my personality began to soften and my mannerisms no longer reflected the stiff, militaristic self-vigilance that had kept me isolated from the circus of life in New Orleans. As I became more comfortable with this new image of myself, I met some new friends, which opened other doors of opportunity.

When Dave grew tired of having a houseguest, he introduced me to a friend of his who was moving out of an apartment. I was able to stay there for the five weeks left on the lease and pay my way by patching and painting the walls, making the apartment ready for a new tenant. The apartment was more centrally located in the *Schawbing* district, on the other side of the *Englisher-Garten* from where Dave lived and near the *Leopoldstasse* and the university. Between irregular working hours at my job with the catering firm and painting the walls of the apartment, I spent time writing in my journal, taking leisurely walks through the park and wasting frigid afternoons in quiet little pastry shops, drinking coffee and eating Bavarian pastries. It was on one such afternoon that I met Rudolph.

I was sitting in a café in *Citta 2000*—a fashionable mini-mall on the Leopoldstrasse modeled on *Le Drugstore* in Paris, with several floors of boutiques, restaurants and cafes. I was reading the Herald Tribune, trying to look casual and chic. My clothes, fitting my new Europeanized self-image, were more urbane—corduroy pants with a wool sweater, and my hair was now long enough to reach the collar of my shirt. I sat with my legs crossed at the knee—not ankle-on-thigh, as my father had taught me—sipping a cappuccino and watching the people in the mall. When I glanced over the top of my newspaper, I saw him. Rudolph possessed that striking combination of handsome blond-haired, blue-eyed Aryan features and a vague familiarity that caused both men and women to turn their heads discreetly and take a second look. As though his classic good looks were not enough to draw attention to himself, he was covered from shoulder to ankle in a 1930s style beaver fur coat. A sudden film-clip image of an antiquated Hollywood icon flashed through my mind, which made me smile. Seeing me smile, his eyes locked onto mine and would not let go until he was sitting beside me, sipping tea and exercising the elocution of his English conversation skills.

At first, he made me a little nervous, this stranger who barged so brashly into my private space. I felt my sphincter tighten automatically, as it does when the ego's integrity is threatened by intrusion. But when he told me his name, I had to stifle a chuckle. "Like Rudolph Valentino?" I asked.

He smiled knowingly, as though the comparison was one that he had often heard, and continued, unflinching, with our conversation. When he told me he was an actor from Berlin on his way home from making a film in Yugoslavia, my inquisitiveness was satisfied enough to accept in him qualities that I might have considered peculiar in another. He no longer seemed so threatening. Rudi—that's what his friends called him—rambled on about this and that, talking directly into my eyes until he was certain that something inside me was listening, not to his words, but to the soft melody of his voice.

His interest in me intrigued rather than disturbed my sense of masculinity. He was gentle in a way that seemed to emanate from an inner essence, and that gentleness reached out to subdue me. He penetrated my ego defenses, bringing a sudden feeling of joy that rose from inside and drew a shy smile on my face. I relaxed and let him caress my soul. I could erect barriers to the outside world when I needed to, but I did not want to defend myself from Rudi's influence. He was communing with my soul, without shame and without restraint. He was seducing me.

Being seduced by another male was not an unfamiliar experience. There was my first sexual experience at the age of sixteen with my neighbor, and I had visited gay bars in Chicago when I was in college and home on leave from the army. That is, I had submitted to both homo- and hetero-experimentation, but I was never very satisfied by the experiences. Anonymous, casual sex did not satisfy me because it did not touch me deeply. Now this stranger in Munich was touching my soul. Not only was I willing to let him seduce me, I wanted him to.

Outside, the night had grown dark and still. It was too cold to be walking, though there was a normal flow of automobile traffic on the Leopoldstrasse. Rudi insisted that we walk. He pointed out things of interest, maintained a flow of conversation, gently directed my attention by touching my arm and made me respond to his advances with a radiant flash from his eyes. It made me shiver. But then, when we arrived in front of the Four Seasons Hotel where he was staying, his mood shifted and the look on his face suddenly changed. I thought he was going to say goodbye and did not want him to leave me standing alone in the cold.

For a long moment he said nothing. He did not disguise his desire. Yet, with the same subtlety of gesture that had characterized his treatment of me all evening, he indicated that he did not intend to compromise me. Through the silence I felt something warm and gentle and nurturing in his masculinity—something that was comforting, something that I wanted to respond to, something that I needed. Finally, he smiled and asked if I wanted to come up to his room. Without hesitation, I said, "yes."

The room was large—made warm and glowing by the gold, beige and brown décor. We removed our coats and sweaters and sat on the edge of the bed caressing each other with our eyes. His silk shirt, open at the collar, was as smooth as the skin beneath and I watched his nipples rise and fall against the silk with each breath that, like my own, became heated with the fire of our passion. I touched him and slipped my hand beneath his shirt. His arms already around my neck, he pulled me close and our lips met, wet and sweet, while our hands fumbled with each other's zippers until, holding each other and kissing, we fell back, laughing, on the bed.

Then, with more deliberation, Rudi took charge and I submitted to his lead. We slowly finished undressing each other. He wanted to take a shower before we made love, and we stood for a long time beneath the steamy water, soaping and kissing, finding the sensitive caresses that gave us both great pleasure. Then we fell onto the bed and made love. Rudi's caresses did not awaken the fiery, aggressive passion of the warrior spirit, but a gentler passion, born out of the steamy waters of my soul.

He stayed in Munich for another week. When I wasn't working, we made love in the afternoon in his hotel room. In the evening, we had dinner in elegant restaurants and he showed me a side of the city and the culture to which there was no access without an intimate guide.

Rudi was five or six years older than me, worldly and sophisticated, already an established stage and film actor. He knew all the right places to go, and introduced me to some of the many people he knew in the film industry. He was showing me off to his friends and I, though somewhat naïve as to how I should conduct myself, absorbed the attention that was lavished upon me. Rudi touched my soul, and I surrendered myself to his touch. With him, I found an intimacy that I had desired for a decade. No matter how fleeting it might prove to be, I wanted to explore that avenue of erotic liberation.

That avenue had opened once before with Mike when we were in New Orleans together. But the timing and circumstances were inappropriate, and the vitality of our souls was stifled by duty, honor and the behavioral expectations imposed on us by the military. Later, when I returned to New Orleans alone, my soul was still in shackles, and I remained an observer, standing on the outside, looking in.

Rudi liberated me from those shackles. As my guide and mentor, he showed me a fantastic undercurrent of people and places more subtly infused with the life and culture of the city than I had found in New Orleans. In Munich, the decadence did not just skim the surface only to bury its guilt in the darkness. It was completely infused into the fabric of the culture as a side of life that emerged from the shadows of the night to balance the stoic self-discipline that the Germans showed to the world in the light of day. Thus, in keeping with the psychological texture of Europe, that balance was an accepted fact of life. Each side kept within its own boundaries. Crossing the boundary from stoicism to decadence was a matter of personal choice, but having made the choice to cross to the other side, one had to relinquish pious indignation. With my curiosity ablaze, I took Rudi's hand and stepped into a world and life that astonished my senses.

We found that life in closed-door, private clubs where Rudi was well known and welcomed by the door guards—the guardians of the boundary. Those unobtrusive doors on quiet streets near the *Sendlinger Tor* opened into splendid cabarets, with all the fashion and glitter of an exclusive nightlife where people reveled in all of the excesses of their Eros spirits. The patrons were the rich, the fashionable and the artistic. Voluptuous young women, courtesans who were paid for their pleasures, flirted with men and with each other. Respectable older gentlemen in business suits, with a drink in one hand, ran the other over the smooth asses of girls young enough to be their daughters or granddaughters. Wealthy dowagers, sparkling with jewels, openly fondled the crotches of their young gigolos. Gay aristocrats sat in dark corners kissing the necks and stroking the boners of the adolescent boyfriends on their laps.

They were all the types I had met on the streets of New Orleans, but the whores sipped champagne and wore jewels provided by their clients. Boys only a few years younger than me were there not to sell their promiscuity but to give it away in exchange for the laughter and the frivolous indulgences of youth. There were effeminate men, young and old, but there were no shrieking Tinkerbelles.

During that week I spent with Rudi, I explored another aspect of my masculinity that was different from the soulless, competitive egoism that had served as a model in my youth. But too, it was different from the neurotic travesty that I had encountered among gays in the United States. In Rudi, there was no contradiction, no masculine and feminine spirits struggling to dominate the personality. He was a homoerotic male. He expressed his masculinity in a way that was strong without being chauvinistic; he was gentle, sensitive and erotic without being effeminate. His artistic occupation gave him license to express himself in a way that he might not have had in another profession, and by his openness in showing me that world, he extended that license to me. When he had to return to Berlin, it was a sad farewell for both of us. We said our goodbye on the street in front of his hotel without an outward display of emotion, though tears glistened in the corners of both our eyes.

A few weeks later he called, invited me to come to Berlin to spend Christmas with him and sent me an airline ticket. I flew up a few days before Christmas. Rudi met me at the airport and took me directly to his apartment where we fell on the bed and made love. Once again, I felt secure in his arms. He had a few days off from his work and showed me his city with an almost adolescent excitement and enthusiasm that was tempered with suave sophistication—a mixture of moods typical of one ensconced in his own comfortable surroundings.

On Christmas Eve we attended a lavish dinner party in the elegant apartment of one of Rudi's gay friends. There were only eight guests for the traditional midnight meal of a Christmas Goose with trimmings. The apartment was spacious and impeccably decorated with three main entertaining rooms. The first was a formal salon. Then there was the dining room, which, though most rooms are rectangular, was perfectly square with a large, round table in the center set for eight. A golden chandelier hung from the ceiling. A rich fabric of red brocade covered the walls, and an elegantly carved oak sideboard, built into the wall, defined the lower part of three walls of the room.

The third room where the guests were gathered was an informal salon decorated in a Moroccan style. There were low benches with lots of silk cushions around the walls. Moroccan rugs covered the parquet floor, and a chandelier hung from a high ceiling so that the light from within the fixture shown through star-shaped holes and cast fuzzy stars against the dark ceiling.

The guests, all male couples, sipped drinks and smoked a pipe of hashish that was being passed around the room. Rudi and I took our place next to a fine looking, gray haired gentleman, probably in his mid fifties, and his adolescent boyfriend. While Rudi and his friend conversed in a rapidly spoken German that I could not follow, I stared with curiosity at the boy who, even though obviously stoned, had the beauty of an angel. He looked back at me with a wry smile. When someone turned up the music on the stereo, far from feigning jealousy, Rudi and his friend smiled at us and encouraged us to dance together. I took a few more hits on the hash pipe. As the youngest two at the party, I sensed that we were being invited to provide an erotic spectacle for the older men who were enjoying watching us dance together under the star-lit chandelier—just a little before-dinner-tease to make the erotic atmosphere tingle a little bit. The boy and I only touched, but we did not speak to each other, and I never knew his name. The music ended and we kissed. Dinner was announced.

I only stayed in Berlin for about five days. As soon as the Christmas holiday was over, Rudi's mood changed perceptibly, as he had to report back to work. He was beginning rehearsals for a new play, which made him tense and nervous and, even on that first day, I could tell that his passions were exhausted by the demands of the role. We smoked a little hash and slept together, curled up naked in each other's arms, but Rudi's immersion in his work left no room in his life for a lover. I had been a diversion for him between jobs. When he took me to the airport for the flight back to Munich, it was not a tearful separation but one of mutual understanding and, I hoped, mutual respect. I had learned a lot from Rudi about myself, but staying with him would have been an unwelcome distraction for him and would have distracted me from my own path.

Back in Munich, I found a new job working construction on the site of the 1972 Olympiad. I moved from the apartment in *Schwabing* into a company barrack near the job site and settled into a work schedule that would allow me to save enough money to travel through Italy and Greece in the spring. There was little time to enjoy the debonair nightlife. However, Rudi had taken me to one club that I particularly liked and several times during the pre-Lenten *Fasching Fest*, I returned there alone. I was as welcome by the guardians at the door as I had been when Rudi first introduced me.

Inside, the décor had changed from a holiday mood to that of *Carnival*. Some of the patrons came in costumes and masks, but all were there to revel in the pagan Dionysian madness that preceded the sober tranquility of the forty days of Catholic Lent. Strobe lights and disco music accompanied dancers who stripped atop cylindrical pedestals beneath hot, flashing lights. In one room, the dancing girls were located behind an enormous curved bar. They stripped down to sequined G-strings and sequined pasties on their nipples, and used their hands to bathe their bodies in the vibrations of the music. They did not look directly at the audience but closed their eyes, smiling and sway-ing seductively in a detached, autoerotic trance that reached across the dream-space separating them from the audience, arousing fantasies in the imaginations of patrons who were lavishly lubricated with alcohol.

More personable, the dancing boys in the other room were not sequestered. Fully clothed, supple youths in their late teens mounted tall cylinders placed in the middle of the dance floor. Moving to the rhythm of the music, they stripped to shimmering codpieces with seductive aplomb. They pumped their arms to the music and thrust their smooth, young bodies toward the audience with smiles that were neither shy nor hidden in trances, but openly solicitous of a homoerotic rapport with the patrons who delighted in the revelation of their young, athletic physiques.

Those gyrating bodies tugged at my senses, challenging my rational self-control with a sensuous, persuasive invitation to plunge once more into the exploration of my own erotic vitality. As the music, the feelings and the alcohol enveloped me, the masked faces of other patrons in the room began to swirl, seeming to taunt the restraints of civil morality, loosening its grip until I was able to reach out and touch them with my passion. After all, it was Carnival, a time to let loose the restraints of civilized culture, to don a mask of anonymity, to pass over the boundary between propriety and decadence and, for a few days each year, revel in the Dionysian excesses of the Eros spirit.

I stumbled back to my lodging, drunk and frustrated by the unrequited seduction of my evening in the pleasure palace, and fell asleep. Stirred by the eroticism and sensuality of the evening, my dreams started innocently enough. There was a dance floor with many streaming, writhing bodies gyrating around me beneath a flashing strobe light. But my inner spirit was not so amused. What awoke in me was not the soft whisper of the Eros spirit, seduced by those dancing bodies, but the darker passion of the warrior, evoked by envy and frustration. In my dream a dark figure broke onto the dance floor with a pistol and started shooting. The shadowy figure walked up to the girl with whom I was dancing, pointed the pistol at her head and fired. Then he turned and looked directly at me. I woke up panting in a sweat. To me, the symbolism was clear. The girl that I was dancing with in my dream was the softer, gentler side of my own personality: my soul. The shadowy figure was the spirit of death and, at last, we had come face to face.

The dream that had begun with erotic exuberance had turned into a bloodbath to gratify the wounded spirit of the warrior. The ungratified blood lust resurfaced to deprive me of love and ecstasy—the two emotions that, apparently, I was still under some order to control.

It was then that I realized how significant, how vital my relationship with Rudi had been. He was the strong, comforting soul that cooled the still raging fire of my frustrated warrior. I stopped going to the cabaret. Perhaps for others crossing into that decadence represented an ecstatic release from the disciplined pressures of social propriety. But in crossing the boundary from the stoic self-discipline of the ego into the mysterious landscape of the soul, one also encounters the shadows—the dark side that can engulf a personality or an entire culture. I simply could not afford that luxury.

Though I did not return to the clubs, one winter night I discovered the opera—a cultural form that was new to me and helped me develop a different perspective on the warrior's transformation. My senses thrilled to the grandiose sweep of emotions portrayed in the scenery, costumes and music that filled the opera house, bringing to life the heroic legends of Western civilization—the Grail heroes, Parsifal and Lohengrin, and Siegfried, the Germanic hero of Wagner's opera, *The Ring of the Nibelungen*. I felt a strong empathy with those tortured heroes, for their eternal contest confirmed that the gods did, indeed, inflict frail mortals with the burdens of divine passion. Learning how to contain those passions was the hero's journey of initiation. The warrior spirit did not have to serve death, if it sought its own heroic transformation.

It was then that I began to realize how deeply malevolent were the policies of the Vietnam War, where the most important calculation of victory was a body count. *"Waste 'em all!"* was the dispassionate order sent down to the soldiers in the field by commanders safely ensconced in their command posts. *Search-and-destroy* missions were missions of total destruction. Those policies condemned the whole of American society, because they turned the courageous warrior spirit, willing to confront death in order to save his loved ones or his country from destruction, into the mindless actions of a mechanized soldier. That condemnation was pronounced most dramatically in the spring of 1971, with the final days of the trial and subsequent conviction of Lt. William Calley for his participation in ordering the massacre at My Lai.

✫ ✫ ✫

The massacre had taken place in March of 1968, just weeks before my helicopter crashed. The "Incident at My Lai," as the media called, did not come to the attention of the news media until 1969. Calley's court martial took place during the winter of 1970-71 and the final verdict was announced in the spring.

In my lodging near the job site of the Olympiad, I listened to the progress of the trial on Armed Forces Radio. A lot was said about the culpability of the chain of command, but what was not discussed was that the massacre had been a direct result of the gook syndrome that was instilled in all of us as an integral part of our training as soldiers.

The gook syndrome implanted the subtle idea that all the Vietnamese were the enemy, and killing civilians was justified by the theory underlying the policy of *free-fire-zones*. The syndrome was really a conditioned hatred of the people and their culture that justified the free reign of the god of death. That hatred undermined the heroic dimension of the warrior's personality and corrupted his ability to abide by a code of morality agreed among warriors.

That is what had happened to Steve, the scout pilot in Vietnam whose place I took on the day of my crash. Steve was in a situation where he had only to allow the moral conscience of the warrior to step forward and instruct him on what to do with the old man he was interrogating. But he panicked. The moral code of the warrior broke down and the dependency of the mechanized soldier, eager only to be given and carry out orders, took its place. He had succumbed to the dark, shadow side of the warrior's personality and, rather than confronting and conquering death, he became its instrument. It seemed to me that that, too, was what had happened to all of the men who participated in the massacre at My Lai.

That was the insidious mechanism inherent in the mechanization of the soldier. Certainly there were soldiers who did not succumb to the perversion of the warrior's morality, but every soldier in Vietnam had to struggle with that perversion day after day. And when the morality of the warrior spirit broke down through errors in command decisions or lack of communication, or when reason was overwhelmed by irrational fear, the result was murder—like Steve killing the old man, like the massacre at My Lai. Listening to the trial of William Calley, I suddenly felt as though the blinders had been taken from my eyes. For the first time I really understood the significance of my own struggle with the killer-instinct.

Easter Sunday arrived with a brilliant sunrise that dispelled the gloom of overcast skies that had hung over the city for several days. Instinctively, I reached up and turned on my radio, always tuned to the English language Armed Forces station. That morning, as part of their Easter Sunday service, they broadcast in full and uninterrupted the Broadway musical, *Jesus Christ, Superstar.* As I listened to the music and lyrics they stirred something deep inside of me. For the first time in four years, I realized how lucky I was never to have had the opportunity to take another human life. The Guardian Angel that had plucked me so dramatically out of the combat zone had saved me from that stain on my soul. I got down on my knees and—probably for the first time since I had stopped going to regular church services as a teenager—said the Lord's Prayer.

Then I wept. It was a deep, emotional lamentation that welled-up, uncontrollably, from deep inside. I remembered Steve, standing beneath the flashing rotor-blade of his scout ship. I wondered what had happened to him and said a brief prayer for him, too. I also thought about William Calley, who was so unabashedly possessed by the god of death, and I tried to have compassion for him as well, but I could not find it. I kept seeing in my mind's eye that burned little girl in tears running naked down the road. I wept for a long time. I wept for all of the victims of that nasty war. I wept for all of my comrades-in-arms who had committed suicide since returning from Vietnam. And with my sobs I was finally able to loosen the unrelenting grip of the killer-instinct that had held such a powerful influence on my soul and on my life.

CHAPTER EIGHT:

Athens

It had been nearly four years since the killer-instinct had gripped my soul. The weight of that burden had made me look older than my twenty-five years. Now, with new revelations awakened in me by the My Lai trail and the brilliant Easter Sunday broadcast, I had wrestled free from the desire to take a human life and a new flower blossomed in my soul. During my last months in Munich, those changes affected the way I felt about myself, and my physical appearance.

Already, as a result of doing heavy construction, my body was thinner and harder than it had been during my years in the military. Working construction put a fresh vigor in my muscles that I felt as a new strength and lightness-of-being that flowed easily into my reawakened youthfulness. Not only had I put the desire to kill behind me, it seemed as though I had regressed to a point before the military and the war had entered my life. I felt that my new experiences now merged with those of adventurous young travelers who were just starting out on their journey in life. I was being given a second chance.

To express that youthful freedom reborn in my soul, I let my brown hair, lightly streaked with silver, grow so that it flowed nearly to my shoulders, but I kept it clean and fashionably cut. I wore a Moroccan bead on a leather thong around my neck—a gift from Rudi. My shirts were open down to the forth button in the fashion of young Italians, and I wore new well-cut corduroy pants and new suede boots. My appearance now conformed to the fashion-conscious self-image that, along with my new attitude, was in keeping with what I felt to be the psychological texture of Europe.

Additionally, my self-esteem, which had been at a low point when I arrived in Europe, got a boost when I received a letter of acceptance from the London School of Economics to study for a graduate degree in philosophy. I had not yet heard from Oxford, but there was still time before making a final decision about which university to attend. The acceptance letter reinforced my determination to stay in Europe, at least until the end of the war, and gave me the excuse I needed to dissolve the bonds that kept me tied to my self-image as an American.

I was still angry at America. The strongest feeling I had about the society that had sent me to war and corrupted my soul was a sense of abandonment. Vietnam veterans were caught in the middle of a civilian society that had not sacrificed to support the war effort but was split over it. We were not going to be welcomed back into the community until the war was over and the split healed. That was a good enough reason for me to stay in Europe.

In the United States, I would have been treated as just another wounded warrior for whom there was little empathy or tolerance, and I did not have the support system that would give me the freedom to explore new experiences that I needed to cleanse and heal my soul. Maybe hippies had found that freedom, but I was not a hippy. As for the *equal pursuit of opportunity* that was so ingrained in the American creed, it seemed no more available to me, a Vietnam War veteran, than it was to those who were disenfranchised by race, ethnicity or gender. Alienated from those things that defined an ideal Americanism, I already had been driven into exile.

I thrust myself head first into the new problem of reinventing myself by questioning everything I had ever learned about the American character. My father had instilled in me the character building virtues consistent with the American identity of a strong work ethic, a sense of Emersonian self-reliance and the drive of self-determination. He had also instilled in me his sense of rational pragmatism from which I concluded that self-determination is governed by a willful, competitive ego. *You can be anything you want to be, if you have the determination to fight for it,* was generally what my father told me all the years I was growing up. Now I was beginning to realize that egoism conflicts with the deeper, intrinsic sense of self characterized by the soul. Egoism exemplifies the attitude—molded into the American character—that the formation of one's identity is motivated by self-interest.

Of course, the objective of e*nlightened* self-interest is to pursue individual fulfillment while contributing to the common good. But it seemed to me that the "enlightened" part of self-interest had become corrupted. Individual success, rewarded with fame and riches, did not necessarily benefit the common good or accrue the good will of society and its blessing. And it seemed as though ruthless egoism was celebrated, even though it often carried with it a load of psychological burdens.

That is what the counterculture revolution of the 60s and 70s was rebelling against. A whole generation began looking for the deeper, spiritual foundations of the personality—some in communes, some in religious movements and some through drugs. That new attitude was, in fact, the trademark of a whole generation in the process of reinventing itself and, after my years in the military, I was drawn easily to that quest. Already, I knew that my soul was too sensitive to be buried under the shell of competitive egoism—something that my father never understood about me but which my mother, had she lived, would have nurtured. Now, I would have to nurture it in myself.

As it turned out, my repudiation of my national identity was a blessing that forced me to look back through the shroud of forgotten generations to the roots of my cultural heritage as a European-American. I seized the opportunity to discover my own intrinsic sense of being and explore the depths of my European heritage, which lay with the English, Scots and Irish and their more primitive foundations in Celtic culture and the classic cultures of Rome and Greece.

As I absorbed the psychological texture of Europe, I found myself relating to my cultural heritage on a sensitive rather than an intellectual level. But I also began making critical comparisons between the multiculturalism of American society and the common cultural themes of different European societies. Though the European Union was young, I also discovered that Europeans, too, were exploring those common cultural themes.

It seemed to me that in Europe individuals were tied together in a cultural fabric that was not so much rationally defined—as it was in multicultural America—but more unconscious, tribal and intrinsic to their nature. That is, cultural identity—whether English, German or French—was more a quality of the soul, like that which I had detected in my relationship with Rudi. That different sense of cultural identity affected the individual's sense of self-determination and self-reliance so that Europeans were not as blatantly individualistic as Americans.

Thus it seemed to me that the European character possessed more balance between the mysterious cultural-connectedness of the soul and the existential alienation of the ego. Self-conscious individuality was balanced with an immutable, unconscious cultural heritage that tempered aggressive self-determination. That cultural connectedness gave everyone a stronger sense of individual identity but also a shared responsibility to remain conscientious of what benefited the whole society. As a result of that inherent sense of social responsibility, individual endeavor received a benign collective blessing.

Though the necessity to reinvent myself caused me to look at the European character through rose-colored glasses, I was not ignorant of history. European tribalism had spawned centuries of warfare, and the collective cultural heritage of Europe had its own demons, so recently exemplified by fascist dictatorships, and ingrown rigidities against which young people in Europe also were rebelling. But the opportunity to make those comparisons with my American identity changed my way of looking at the world.

As I became more comfortable with a view of reality centered closer to the soul than to the ego, I was prepared to immerse myself completely in the culture heritage of my European forefathers. I had spent these months in Germany because that is where I could get working papers. But now I was already beginning to plan how I would explore my Celtic roots in the British Isles once I was settled into an English university. For the moment, carried away by these new revelations about my European cultural heritage, I wanted to dig further back in time to the ancient origins of European culture. I needed to go to Greece.

In April, I quit my construction job in Munich and crossed the Brenner Pass on a train to Venice. I planned to travel down the Italian coast by train and cross the Adriatic Sea to the land of my spiritual ancestors, the land where perhaps I would discover the origins of my soul.

✫ ✫ ✫

In contrast to the public stoicism of the German character, the Mediterranean climate and geography seemed to combine in a way that charged the character of the people with emotion and feeling. I spent several days in Venice, fortunate to have arrived in early spring, before the summer heat caused the canals to smell of garbage and the populace, tired of summer tourists, grew reclusive. The weather was warm and sunny, and each day made me more aware of a vibrant atmosphere that was both sensual and seductive.

Through the newly opened portals of my receptive soul, I took in the passionate expressions of Italians going about their daily activities. While buying a fresh mozzarella that hung in a vendor's open stall in the market, I witnessed an emotional exchange between a middle-aged, mustachioed grocer and a dumpily, irate customer. Hands and arms flailed and faces grimaced with expression. I did not understand the words that, for all I knew, might have only defended the price of a head of lettuce. But the passion and lyrics of the language sang in my ear with a rhythm that also could have been an operatic aria. Expressions, feelings and gestures leapt across the space between the actors and me, an audience of one, penetrating my sensitivities and alerting my soul to the thrust and parry of the contest that ended with a soothing word, a smile and the *clink* of lire in the cash register.

A seductive young woman with long black hair crossed the *Piazza San Marcos* in stiletto heels. Her red, silky dress clung and then swayed with the movement of her body beneath the garment. She left an arc of perfume in the air that followed behind her and drifted toward where I sat in a café sipping coffee. Suddenly, it seemed to gather in a cloud when she stopped, turned her head as though looking for someone, then moved on, carrying grace, the perfume and the silky movement of her dress within the subtle language of her body.

The sound of a mandolin floated on the air, where I sat in a small neighborhood *piazza* reading the Herald Tribune and eating a pastry. A schoolboy wearing dark shorts and a full white blouse stopped his bicycle by the fountain. I stared at him. He stretched his bare leg to the cobblestone, threw his dark curls casually to one side and glared back at me with black eyes. Then his soft lips curled his smooth cheeks into a bright smile and he rode away, knowing he had touched my soul.

It was as though the whole world was aware of its own provocative sensuality and embraced the perceptive one as one of its own. In an atmosphere charged with nuance, suggestion and symbolism, I opened myself to the stir of emotions that spiraled down into the depths of my being, not as an invader but as a friend, gently persuading me to reveal and carry the weight of my own sensuality—my own connectedness to the world. Confronted with the awe-inspiring power that reached inside and drew me out of myself, I fell more deeply into the embrace of the mystery of my own soul. My abstract warrior spirit did not protest, and my masculine ego let itself succumb to the eternal feminine power that resided within me. As that provocative sensuality awakened, a new and mysterious energy began to flow outward, transforming my image in the looking glass of self-reflection, transforming the person that I had always thought myself to be.

It could have been a frightening experience. Fear could have prevented me from peering further into the mysterious depths of those dark corridors deep within myself. But any fear I had gave way to an almost unrestrained curiosity to explore the side of myself that was mysterious, yet oddly familiar—a part of myself that, since early adolescence, had been buried in self-consciousness. I let that desire grow and, after a few days, I was ready to proceed toward that small and hidden doorway that leads inward to the mysterious landscape of the soul, where all things, places and people are made richer by their resonance with symbolic meaning. It was time to move on to Greece.

☆ ☆ ☆

I skipped Rome and took a train that followed the Adriatic Coast south through Rimini, Ancona, Bari and Brindisi. There, I boarded a ship for a quiet, night-journey that turned into a sunlit day on a calm sea, beneath puffy, white clouds drifting through an azure dome. We passed Corfu—Odysseus' Ithaca—and sailed the Ionian Sea down to Patra, where buses were waiting to take the boat passengers on to Athens.

All along the route those things that were essentially strange and new—bouzouki music playing on the bus, the arid countryside along the coastline of the Gulf of Corinth, the lamb roasting on the open spit where the bus stopped for a noonday meal of gyros, Greek salad and beer—all felt remarkably comfortable and familiar in a strange and mysterious way. By the time I arrived in Athens, my soul sparkled with the joy of returning to a familiar homeland and anticipation of what lay ahead.

It was the city of the goddess Athena, whose magnificent statue had once stood guard on the Acropolis holding a warrior's spear, adorned with a warrior's helmet and carrying the emblem of Medusa on her breastplate and on her shield. She was not a classic nurturing goddess, but a warrior, born not of a mother but fully clothed out of the split-open head of Zeus. She was the goddess of wisdom but she carried with her the emblem of a demon-woman who could turn to stone the men who gazed upon her.

I found a small hotel near *Omonia Square*, within walking distance of the ruins of the *Parthenon* and the *Agora,* where I spent my days wandering among the shades of Athens' former glory. With the channel to my soul completely opened, I gained a new appreciation for the antiquity of Western civilization.

Since high school, I had been enthralled with ancient Greece. Its gods and warrior heroes remained familiar. Now, among the ruins of the ancient city, I could *feel* what, before, had only been an abstract, intellectual image. Now what my father called an *over-active* imagination, to be kept in check by my developing intellect, at last could be set free. I could feel the timeless entity of the warrior spirit rising up within me to meet the primordial icons from which it originated.

My warrior spirit had been out of place in Vietnam—uncomfortable and incongruent in the mechanized war in Southeast Asia. And I was only a spectator to the warrior heroes—Parsifal, Lohengrin and Siegfried—who marched across the operatic stage in Munich. But in Athens, my warrior spirit danced a new life, remembering what it had been like when Odysseus, Achilles and Alexander had crossed the world-stage, leaving a resonance in their wake that could not be disguised by toppling the temples and raising the skyscrapers. The eternal resonance remains for those whose souls are sensitive to the timelessness of the mystic vibration. Those vibrations filled my mind with images—visions of the life that had once thrived among the ruins. As I moved through the same space where ancient warriors had once walked, I felt their spirits coursing through the sinews of my body, displaced by twenty-five centuries, yet *not* bound by the lonely condition of time's displacement. The cool, dry spirit-wind, blowing down from high Olympus, still had the power to awaken the gods that slept in the mystic realm. Now as I climbed over the toppled stones and walked among the high grasses, that spirit-wind touched me.

I sensed the crowds of Athenians crammed together in the narrow alleyways of the Agora, talking and jostling and laughing as they went about their daily business. Stalls of merchants and artisans lined the path. Painters and sculptors worked there. Dancers and musicians practiced there. A poet taught his pupils the subtle movement and inflection of his drama, conducting his business in the Agora while the crowds passed by, occasionally stopping to listen, but not interfering with his lesson. Men stood talking of philosophy or politics. Boys and young men sat on the ground and leaned against the walls, listening to a teacher who sat on a stoop, his white, linen mantle draped around his waist, his arm raised and his finger pointing to gesture, his eyes sparkling, hypnotizing his students with the wisdom of his words.

Socrates had trod there once. He was surrounded by an entourage of inquisitive young men eager to be touched by the charisma that tumbled from his lips in a mellifluous flow of questions that punctured their delicate egos and stirred their souls so that they followed his voice, the gesture of his hand, the flow of his robe as he moved along the portico toward his morning appointment in the gymnasium. There, naked youths exercised in the warm Attic sun. Afterward, they bathed with oil, scraped each other's bodies and smiled over their shoulders with flashing eyes at the barefoot old man wrapped in a white mantle who knew the names of the gods that attended their spirits and addressed himself to the Eros-lover in their souls.

Socrates spoke of the soul's journey through eternity. *If the soul does not die with the body but goes on as a thing immortal, then, is it not true that a part of immortality lives within us? Then, is it not also true that whatever the soul occupies, she comes to bringing life?*

I was trying to imitate Socrates' voice, and the eternal words from *Phaedo* resonated like the tingling of a wind-chime in the gentle caress of a mystical breeze. *Then, because she is immortal, does not the soul know everything? Learning is only remembering what the soul within us already knows.*

When death approaches a man, is it not true that the mortal part of him dies? But then, one might conclude that the immortal part of him goes away undestroyed, guided by Hermes toward its place in the underworld until the time comes for it to be reborn. Then, it is guided back into a new life, forgetting all that went before but ready to remember, again, what it has always known.

I was eager to remember.

Beside the ancient Agora, on the porch of the reconstructed *Portico of Attalus,* stood a statue of Hermes holding the baby Dionysus on his shoulder—a white marble statue standing dramatically against a blood-red, stucco wall. The guide of souls, messenger of the gods, was fused with the infant form of that powerful, lusty spirit whose duty it was to awaken the human soul to its own myriad of ecstatic possibilities. The innocent looking child cupped his hand and whispered lusty thoughts into the ear of the youthful psycho-pomp. Hermes responded with blank, white marble eyes that stared into mine. I smiled at the words I heard in my inner ear—a secret message from Dionysus-Hermes that was conveyed on a spirit-wind that stirred the air and threw a wisp of dust around my feet.

The following day, still nudged along by the spirit-wind that followed mystic channels down from high Olympus and flowed through the open portals of my sensual mind, I found myself in the corridors of the National Gallery. I passed the tall Greco-Egyptian *Kouros* statue of the early archaic period with only a nod of courtesy, and walked swiftly through a long gallery toward the far corner of the building.

Set in a square hall defined by the showcases of other displays, stood the magnificent *Poseidon-of-Artimision.* I was filled with awe and recognition of that sculpture of a man, a god-length larger than life. He was covered with a fine skin of emerald patina, and every detail of the finely crafted bronze casting remained intact, though it had rested beneath the sea for two thousand years. Only the eyes were empty—the ivory and jewel eyes that, for all who would see the bronze statue, depicted the quality of the soul. Now, he stood naked and empty in defiance of time—a witness to the eternity of the gods. The feet and legs were firmly planted. The torso was trim and forceful. The arms were set in a gesture to aim and throw…what?

Those who had discovered the statue called it Poseidon, because it lay beneath the sea. But there were those archeologists who believed that the statue actually depicted Zeus, thus the question of whether he would have been holding a trident or a lightening bolt. What I imagined was that the statue really represented a subtle merger of two brother gods. As such, it suggested a profound revelation about the evolution of the soul that took place in the ancient Greek culture.

In the modern equation of mythology and psychology Poseidon, as ruler of the sea, is the symbolic ruler of the unconscious—the mysterious realm of the inner self. Zeus, from his home on high Olympus, rules over the light of consciousness, the mind of man. I imagined that the sculptor, in a moment of deep intuition, guided by the muse of his inner vision, had a profound insight and merged the two gods. He created a symbolic representation of the fusion of the conscious and unconscious to form a whole being. For me, the statue was symbolic of the wholeness that I sought in myself. In it, I recognized the image of a spiritual father and uncle, stepping across time to remind me that wholeness required an inward journey through the mysterious realm of the soul, through the realm of the feminine within.

My eyes turned toward the deep waters of Poseidon's realm, and I prepared myself for the journey. Already, my intimate encounters with the Eros spirit had led me away from socially conditioned egoism toward a new awakening. I prayed that the spirit-wind would fill and guide me, erasing the blemish of my frustrated initiation and disclose a new and fuller purpose of my selfhood.

That day at the museum was my last day in the city. Though I had only spent a few days in Athens, I decided to leave and seek the simple life of island people. I had no destination in mind, but I had money in my pocket, and I had the summer months ahead to indulge in an adventure that had already led me inward to the mysterious landscape of the soul. Still, I was cautious, trying to keep my imagination, intuition and feeling-toned perceptions balanced with my rational mind. I would enter the mystical realm of the soul, but I would enter it with my eyes wide open and my self-awareness intact. It was a dangerous journey, but I had arrived at the portal through natural means, not through drugs. I knew that the greatest danger lay in somehow losing control over my ability to surrender to or cautiously withdraw from the experiences I would encounter. With those limitations established, I surrendered myself to the spirit-wind that blew across the landscape of my soul.

CHAPTER NINE:

Crete

I went down to Piraeus. Near the dock where boats left for the islands, I found a café, sat drinking coffee, focused on my inner senses and intuition and waited for the spirit-wind to tell me where to go next. When an announcement was posted for an overnight ship leaving for Heraklion, Crete, I knew instinctively that this was the sign I had been waiting for. I ran for the gangplank and clambered aboard, just as the ship was ready to sail.

Deck passenger was the lowest fare, and I made my way to the upper deck. The engines rumbled to life, and we cruised out to sea across waters that darkened with the lengthening shadows, as the sun set over the Peloponnese. I stood at the rail and looked deep into the water for the face of Poseidon, hoping that the god would give me a sign that I had made the right choice and was on the pathway intended by the spirit-wind. The shadows deepened the tones of the water until the blues and the greens floated together merging into a rich, dark aquamarine. Long ripples of shallow, white surf angled outward from the bow of the ship and dissipated in dark hills and valleys that wandered in patterns over the sea—a veil to hide the inner sanctum of Poseidon's abode.

When the last streaks of daylight followed the sun into the cavern of the night for its passage through the underworld, the ship's lights came on and bouzouki music blasted over the loud speaker. Other passengers mingled on the upper deck. Peasant women with wrinkled faces and toothless grins, dressed in long black dresses, wrapped themselves in black shawls against the wind. They huddled atop piles of assorted baggage with their husbands—peasant men with baggy pants, sheepskin vests and long, curled mustaches. Hippies arranged sleeping bags against the bulkheads to protect themselves from the night wind. I did not want to sleep on the deck and thought that, later, I would find a vacant bench in one of the lounges. For the moment, however, I was content to stay on the deck and make a meal out of the bread, cheese and fruit that I had bought at the market in Piraeus. I only needed a bottle of wine to complete my meal.

As I turned from the rail, I literally bumped into two young American women. I knew immediately that they were Americans because there was nothing of a European, fashion-conscious sensitivity about their appearance. They were both chunky girls with sunburned cheeks, dressed in Bermuda shorts and heavy, over-sized army surplus fatigue jackets that hung limply on their shoulders. Sweaty socks drooped over the tops of their hiking boots, and they carried enormous backpacks that stood high above the wind-tousled hair on their heads. Still, they giggled in such a girlish way that I, too, was infected and began to laugh with them. We apologized awkwardly to each other and began a conversation that led to inviting each other to share our meal, for they had also bought cheese and fruit in the market. We agreed, however, on the necessity for a bottle of wine. I left the girls to watch my gear while I went off on a quest to find it.

Trying to express what I wanted in simple English interspersed with the word *Retsina,* I inquired at both the snack bar and the door of the first-class kitchen, without luck. But then as I was turning away dejected from the kitchen door, a young man in a white jacket asked in English if he could help. I told him what I wanted. He replied that he would bring two bottles of red wine to the upper deck. I thanked him, with some apprehension over his motive for helping me, and returned to the girls.

They had spread a blanket beside the bulkhead and laid out our bread, a large hunting knife, the cheese and fruit. They were full of inquiries about our benefactor, which I could not answer. A few minutes later, he arrived with two bottles of wine, as promised. At that point, he introduced himself as the captain's personal steward and announced that, if we wished to do so, the three of us were invited to dine with the captain in his quarters.

'What luck,' I thought.

But the girls were not so certain, for the way the steward continued to examine them made it clear that I was not the one the captain was interested in. They were suspicious of the captain's motives and began to argue over the insidious implications of the invitation, retelling stories they had heard of unpleasant experiences between vulnerable college girls and lusty Greek men. The steward waited patiently while we made up our minds. I told the girls that it would be impolite to refuse the captain's hospitality and, anyway, I would be there to protect them if, indeed, they needed protection. Finally, they relented, and we accepted the invitation.

The captain lived aboard the vessel. The salon of his apartment was a spacious, wood-paneled room with functional but well-worn leather furniture. There was a long table in the center of the room, covered with a white cloth and already set for dinner with the captain's best china, heavy silver utensils on crisply folded linen napkins and an elegant arrangement of fresh-cut flowers as a centerpiece. Captain Chris, a man perhaps in his early forties, was handsome in his well-fitting uniform. His manners were impeccable. Graciously, he introduced himself in heavily accented English and allayed any suspicion by apologetically explaining that he often invited guests to dinner so that he could practice his English. He invited us to sit, and the steward poured glasses of a much finer red wine than the cheap Retsina. A sumptuous meal of roasted lamb was accompanied by an excellent, silky smooth moussaka and mixed vegetables. Bowls of salad and fruit were brought from the kitchen on silver trays.

As we were wined and dined, Chris dominated the conversation in broken English, but with a natural aplomb that, while a little bit boring, gave not the slightest hint of holding ulterior motives. By the time we had finished the several courses of our meal, accompanied by much wine and ouzo, I was quite drowsy. Chris' attention turned completely to the girls. While they drank and giggled—obviously getting drunk, having fun and not needing my protection—the steward took me to a private guest bedroom and left me to a night of totally luxurious sleep.

When I awoke the following morning, we were already docked in Heraklion. After I showered and had breakfast, which was brought to my room by the steward, I met the girls. Though they, too, had showered and eaten, both were hung-over and looked as drowsy and rumpled as they had the night before. They reported having spent a horrible night being chased around the apartment by Chris. I listened with sympathy and amusement, but I did not apologize for not staying up all night to "protect" them since they clearly seemed able to take care of themselves and certainly had a greater tolerance for alcohol than I did. From my point of view, I still thought of the opportunity as an incredible stroke of luck.

In fact, I began to think that it was more than luck. If I were really listening to the voice of the spirit-wind and following it by taking *that* particular ship, then it seemed logical to me that the rightness of my choice would be confirmed. For me, the luck of having spent the night in the luxury of the captain's apartment was just such a confirmation. It fell into the category of a *synchronistic event*—a meaningful coincidence that linked worldly phenomena with spirits that inhabited the mystic realm. Such events must be orchestrated by powerful and mysterious forces that lie beyond the comprehension of the rational mind.

Furthermore, I imagined that, in having surrendered myself willingly to the spirit-wind, those spirits, perhaps even Poseidon, himself, had taken an interest in *my* journey. The chain of synchronistic events that already had led me from Munich to Crete implied that before me stretched not only an island in the sun but a stage already set for the unraveling of some great mystery.

"Crete's mystery is extremely deep. Whoever sets foot on this island senses a mysterious force branching warmly and beneficially through his veins, senses his soul begin to grow," said the famous Greek writer, Nikos Kazantzakis. I surrendered myself to that mysterious force, allowing the gods to direct the role I would play in *their* drama. I only waited for a script to be thrust into my hands.

✲ ✲ ✲

I went directly from the ship to the ruins of the Minoan palace of *Knossos*, which stood on a hill several miles from the port. By some interpretations, the palace was the fabled labyrinth in which the monstrous Minotaur had been kept. According to legend, Poseidon presented *Minos*—the king and lawgiver of Crete—with a sacred white bull from the sea that was to be sacrificed as a sign that the throne of Minos was bestowed by the god. But Minos could not bear to part with the magnificent animal and substituted another bull for the sacrifice. Poseidon was not fooled. As punishment, Poseidon caused *Pasiphae,* the wife of Minos, to be struck with a divine passion for the beast, and from their union bore a monster with the body of a man and the head of a bull. The monster was kept in the labyrinth, perhaps deep in the dungeon-bowels of the palace.

At that time, Crete was the dominant power of the Eastern Mediterranean. King Minos had won a campaign against the Athenians and demanded that, every eight years he was to be sent seven youths and seven maidens as a tribute. Legend had it that they were sacrificed to the Minotaur.

Theseus, son of Aigeus, the king of Athens volunteered to be part of the tribute. Struck by the beauty and strength of the young prince, the daughter of Minos, Ariadne, vowed to help him. She gave him a sword with which to slay the monster and a ball of string with the instruction that he was to unwind the string as he entered the labyrinth so that he could find his way out again. Theseus slew the Minotaur, and the symbolic union between the bull from the sea and the high priestess of the Great Mother was undone. The goddess-worshiping culture of the Minoans fell.

Mythology and history, however, have been boiled together in the cauldron of the human imagination so that the historical reasons for the fall of the culture have been obscured by time. Yet we do know that the most significant historical event contributing to the destruction of the Minoan civilization was probably the explosion of the volcanic island of Thira, 60 miles away. What followed was a cultural fusion of Minoan Crete with Mycenaean Greece and its pantheon of deities dominated by patriarchal Zeus. But in the primordial past—before the male gods dominated the female goddess and the soul of Western man was dominated by his mind—the mysterious forces, revealed in the story of Theseus and the Minotaur, nourished the soul.

Standing on a wind-swept hill where the great palace of Knossos now stood in ruins, I understood the symbolic significance of that story, and any doubt I had that I was on the pathway laid by the spirit-wind was erased. I was prepared to surrender myself to this quest; this personal drama that I hoped would heal my soul. I closed my eyes and stretched out my arms to embrace the wind. Driven by the heat of the African desert, the wind blew warm and sweet over the southern sea, through the gaps in the mountains and twisted my long hair in front of my face. It flowed around and over my body, lifted and carried me over the island, and my imagination soared in flight to survey the stage set for the drama.

In *The Odyssey,* Homer says, *"Out in the dark blue sea there lies a land called Crete, a rich and lovely land, washed by the waves on every side."* The island possessed a prominent and rugged beauty. Behind Knossos was the long ridge of Mount Jukta that resembled the profile of a sleeping god. Behind that ridge, rising to over 8,000 feet, was the snowcapped peak of Mount Ida. Three mountains formed the backbone of the hundred-fifty-mile long island and harbored high mountain plateaus, garden valleys and deep gorges that descended from their rippled ridges down to the southern sea. In the White Mountains to the west, there were heavily forested slopes where wild goats roamed the outcrops of naked stone above the tree line. The central highlands around Mount Ida sheltered fields of wild flowers. The eastern end of the island, beyond Mount Dikte and the fertile Lesithi Plateau, was stark and arid, sloping to cliffs above the sea.

Prominent beaches, like rough-cut jewels shimmering on a silvery chain of sea-foam, encircled the island. Some were hidden beneath the walls of cliffs and bordered quiet coves with sandy floors and coral castles that were visible through the crystal clear surface of the water. Other beaches were long stretches of white sand, assaulted by the pulsing ebb and rolling splash of the surf as it curled up onto the sand, obscuring—when the sun turned sand and sea to a shimmering surface of shifting light—the line between land and water.

That shimmering strand of silver light surrounding the island was a visionary symbol of the boundary between the light of consciousness and the mysterious poetic depths that lie beneath reason's prosaic eloquence. The mountains rose out of the sea of the unconscious—a three-pinnacled, symbolic mindscape of Minoan culture: its architecture, social organization and economy. Beneath those pinnacles of consciousness, in the labyrinthine depths, dwelt the pathetic, divine creature that united the fertilizing powers of Poseidon's sacred bull from the sea with the Great Mother goddess, the *Cybele* and *Isis* of the ancient world who found a new home on Crete.

The early civilization was fed by the self-sacrifice of those who benefited from its superior organization. But the later Minoans—perhaps grown fat, lazy and drunken with wealth and power—no longer made the self-sacrifices demanded of divine propitiation, and found it easier to sacrifice the children of Athens. That perverted the delicate balance between the goddess, the people and the lawgiver. Great Poseidon had his reasons for destroying Minos. For was it not great earth-shaking Poseidon who caused the eruption of Thira and the tsunami, 3,700 years ago, that destroyed the Minoan culture?

When the Greeks came with their pantheon dominated by masculine gods, the Great Mother goddess was splintered. *Hera,* wife of Zeus, took up the domestic and maternal functions of the goddess. *Hestia* was the guardian of the hearth—the divine fire. In her role as provider and nurturer, *Demeter,* the goddess of grain, was perhaps closest to the Great Mother, and she also guarded the labyrinthine depths that lay beneath the pinnacles of consciousness. *Aphrodite* was the goddess of feelings and passion and sexual desire. *Artemis* was goddess of childbirth and ruler over the wild beasts. But she was also goddess of the moon and, before being disposed by masculine gods, she was goddess of the sun and the primitive *Scythian* model of the Great Mother goddess. Wise and aloof *Athena* was symbolic of divine wisdom. Dark *Persephone* was mistress of the underworld. *Hecate*, the dark and terrifying sorceress, was the devouring mother who takes all life back into herself. And *Medusa*, with her tangled serpent-locks, was ready to take revenge on the masculine dominance of the world by turning men to stone.

The domination of the Great Mother goddess by masculine gods is a dynamic story as old as the story of Adam and Eve and the birth of mental consciousness. It set the stage for the conflict between the magical and mythical feminine powers of the heart and soul and the masculine powers of the mind—a conflict that has dominated 6,000 years of Western civilization and history.

The war spread across the world. Aeneas and his small band of defeated Trojans, undaunted by the powers of the Carthaginian queen,

Dido, settled on the Italian peninsula, stripped the Etruscans of their gods and goddesses, their lands and their treasure and established the Roman Empire. Rome conquered the Celts, defeating the three-faced goddess of the cultures of old Europe—*Grianna*, the Celtic sun goddess, *Morrigan*, the goddess of love and war; and *Brigit*, who represented all three goddesses in one.

Built on the rise and fall of the Roman Empire, the three great Western patriarchies—England, France and Spain—advanced across the sea to wage genocide against the native peoples of the Americas, who guarded the balance between the Great Spirit in the sky and the life-giving Great Mother of the earth.

Then, once more, the warlords of the patriarchy, entranced by their power to dominate the Earth Mother and rape her for her treasure, crossed the sea to destroy Vietnam. Au Co, the Princess of the 36th Heaven, and Lac Long Quan, son of the Dragon King, were the divine parents of a people that lived in harmony with the earth until the battle between the patriarchal Titans of communism and capitalism fell upon their land.

I knew that history defended my logic. What I did not know was the name of the power that had brought me to Crete, the power that thrust those images into my mind to decry the warrior spirit within me. As I sensed the immortality of that spirit, I was suddenly being made vividly aware of its guilt, of its role in all those patriarchal victories over the Great Mother goddess. The moving finger of the cold spirit-wind that blew down from the heavens had written those chapters as "victories" in the biography of the human race. But were they not victories that deepened the festering wound in the soul? Now on Crete, I felt a warmer, damper spirit-wind that made me shiver, a long-forgotten breath that tickled the hairs on the nape of my neck.

I spent that first night on the island in Heraklion, but I had already decided to find a quiet village on the beach where I could contemplate this mystery. The following day, I took a bus across the central plateau of the island to the small village of Agia Galini, on the south coast.

✷ ✷ ✷

The village clung obtrusively to the steep, rocky sides of a narrow valley that ended with a small port sheltered by a seawall, beyond which lay the blue waters of the southern sea. The plaza, about two hundred meters inland from the port, was level and paved with cobblestone. The bus rolled into the center of the plaza and stopped in front of a row of stores and restaurants with outdoor tables. All the buildings were whitewashed to reflect the sun's heat, so the interiors stayed cool during the long hot summer months. All the windows and door trims were painted the same blue color of the sea. Across the plaza, beyond the fountain and a row of small houses on the edge of a shallow gully, there was a grassy hill where goats roamed free—the deep tones of the brass bells that hung around their necks echoing against the silence. A dirt path cut diagonally across the green face of the hill, and led to the sheep grazing meadows above the sea cliffs to the west.

The north side of the plaza was reserved for the church—a small building with its white tower gleaming in the sun, weather beaten doors and crowned with a blue tile dome badly in need of repair that was topped with a small iron cross. Down a narrow street that sloped toward the sea was the port, where several fishing boats bobbed gently at their moorings.

The local police captain, looking stern and efficient with his hands clasped behind his back, circled the plaza in his crisp uniform. He seemed to be inspecting the passengers—as we descended one by one from the bus onto the hot, stone paving—and making mental notes on the comings and goings of the local populace while memorizing the faces of strangers. A few passengers, obviously locals returning from a trip to the city, chatted quietly with relatives who met them, while in the background a cock shattered the stillness with its crowing.

Throwing my heavy backpack down ahead of me, I stepped off the bus, surveyed the square and selected a restaurant where I hoped to find something cool to drink. I chose one with a sign that read *Cleo's* and written in English in small letters underneath, *mom's apple pie*. I settled into a flimsy wire chair and ordered something that resembled sweet, syrupy lemonade.

The bus pulled away. Slowly, the plaza cleared. It was the hottest part of the afternoon and the village was silent, except for the sound of the bells around the necks of the goats and the wind that rustled the tall, stately cypress trees next to the church. An eerie silence encircled the village, setting it in a vortex of timelessness. Unhampered by the hurried rituals of urban life, time was marked only by the slow and silent movement of shadows across the ground that quietly punctuated the moments in the day's ritual activities. Life moved reluctantly forward.

Cleo, who had spoken to me in English when she took my order and served the drink, now sat in the dark shadows at the back of the restaurant working on a piece of embroidery. Another older woman, almost invisibly wrapped in black, her head covered with a black shawl, sat in the shadows facing her, rocking back and forth in her chair. I just sat there absorbing the silence that wormed its way between the molecules of my being and expanded my soul. When it finally occurred to me that the shadows indicated the time to find lodging, I paid my bill and was directed by Cleo to a room in a private house up the road from the plaza.

Evening crept in silently and sat still upon the town.

The following morning, I awoke to the crowing of a rooster and the tinkling of the bells around the necks of the goats. Neither had been interrupted by the sound of a motor since the bus had left the day before. From the yard of the house, the smell of barley bread baking in a large, dome-shaped oven drifted into my room. My landlady, an old peasant woman dressed in black, removed the bread from the oven with a long-handled wooden paddle. When the bread had cooled, she served me a breakfast of thick Greek coffee, the fresh-baked barley bread, sheep's milk yogurt and honey. She said nothing but grinned a toothless grin and giggled when I thanked her for the service, the food and the hospitality in a language she did not understand. As I ate my breakfast on the terrace, she perched on a stool by the arched opening of the beehive oven and watched me with sparkling eyes, silently nodding in response to some inner voice that provided her with mysterious insights about the young American who was staying in her home.

Then I realized that she was reading me. It made me feel just a little uncomfortable. We did not share a common language and had not tried to speak with each other, so whatever she saw in me had no rational foundation, but she read me, nonetheless. I surmised that her ways of knowing were more primitive than language and derived purely from instincts, intuitions and feeling-toned impressions that were, perhaps, more highly developed and telepathic than I could have imagined. It gave me a slightly paranoid sensation to believe that I was being read like an open book and, perhaps, understood by this stranger better than I knew myself.

After I had eaten, I thanked her again for preparing the breakfast, went back to my room, changed, took my beach towel and went exploring. I climbed up and down narrow cobblestone streets lined with white houses pressed against each other. A little boy in short pants, who carried a long stick and did not smile, drove a cow and some goats down the street. I found my way to the port. The men of the village were out to sea in their fishing boats, so the port was nearly empty.

A stone quay along the water's edge with a long-armed seawall that looped around into the open sea, forming a breakwater, defined the port. From the port, there was a narrow path lined with pink-flowering oleander bushes for about a hundred yards. Just beyond the last house in the village, the path squeezed between some large boulders and opened onto a small, clean, white sand beach. There were only a few other tourists, but I only stayed on the beach until the mid-day sun became too intense. Behind the beach, a field of tall grasses waved in the warm, gentle breeze, and a cool stream ran down from the mountain through terraces of olive groves. I continued exploring and returned to my room for a nap during the hottest part of the day.

That night, it became evident that there were a lot more tourists in town than the few foreigners I had already encountered on the beach and when I had dined early, the previous evening. They spilled out of their rooms after the sun went down to eat in one of several outdoor restaurants around the plaza that were hung with lights and reverberated with the sounds of Greek music, to which my ear had become accustomed. There were quiet conversations in English, German, French and Greek. When I had arrived, the day before, I had not seen so many people, but Cleo explained that all the hotels in town—a total of perhaps twenty or twenty-five rooms—were full. Those other tourists—Americans, Canadians and Europeans—were not quite hippies, though some gave the impression of spending their vacation-time on the fringes of the hippy movement. I watched their comings and goings without speaking to them, for I had entered a sublime psychic space dominated by feelings and intuition, and I wanted to be alone. This was my first visit to a peasant village since I had stood—an armored, mechanized warrior—before that waterwheel in Vietnam. In Agia Galini I was beginning to feel not like an invader but more like someone who was welcome, as though I had a mysterious communion with the village. I did not want that communion to be contaminated with idle chatter.

In the village there was an absence of the kinds of modern entrapments that keep the mind poised at the level of self-consciousness. The villagers had absorbed a little technology here and there—electricity, running water and a few telephones, but there didn't seem to be very many television sets, home appliances or automobiles. In Agia Galini the silent, timeless vortex of the village had a hypnotic effect that did not assault my senses but, rather, opened the portals of my mind to a wondrous realm of mystery.

I sensed that the villagers were open to a continuous ebb and flow of energy from the cosmos that gently moved through the inner depths of their beings and expanded as it spread across their souls. In place of the self-conscious ego-façade, it seemed that their entire being was a meeting place where the outer world of material reality mingled—rather than collided—with the inner spirits. Those two worlds glistened in the dark eyes of peasant villagers, like deep holographic images in dark, smoky glass.

In those eyes, I sensed that the world was seen as a synthesis of shadow and substance. Phantom spirits revealed the essence of things, and substance was shifted and reshaped, by nature or by the hands of man, into solid forms that were but the residue of possibilities emerging from the spirit realm. It was the toothless, unprovoked grins of those old peasants that gave me the feeling that they were constantly reacting to the subtle interplay between the spirits and the material world in the realm of the soul—a realm that the rest of us could not, or did not, take the time to see. When they looked at me, I felt as though they were absorbing me in the same way that they seemed to absorb their surroundings, through a kind of telepathic communion with the essence of a thing or a person, like the landlady who crouched grinning and seemed to explore the content of my soul without oral communication.

At first, it made me even more uncomfortable to imagine that the whole village, not just the landlady, was able to read my mind. But then

I began to sense that there was a total, nonjudgmental acceptance of me as I was. Their judgment had to include not only the things that I knew about myself, but also the things that I did not know—the things about me that had never risen up from the depths of my unconscious into self-awareness. It was as though the open portals of my soul communicated things to them directly, without passing through the sentinel of my self-conscious mind. Those peasants formed an image of me out of the residue of possibilities that passed freely out of the depths of my inner spirit.

The sensation of an atmosphere permeated with mysterious forces was enhanced by a marked absence of young people. I saw few children, but the ones I did see were not handsome boys or pretty little girls. Their faces, like the gestures and attitudes of the old people, seemed to carry the weight of the ages, as if these children, too, were inbred with the land and had become as much a part of the landscape as the twisted, gnarled trunks of ancient olive trees. These were not the angelic faces of God's cherubs that were depicted on Northern European churches, but the far more ancient faces of the children of the Earth Mother who had possessed the land long before Adam or Zeus or Christ had awakened the mind of man to the god of consciousness.

Yes, the villagers worshiped Adam's God and Christ in the tiny Greek Orthodox Church, and so, too, they must have acknowledged the transcendent mystery of God's presence in all things. But it seemed that the transcendent mystery of God was accepted here alongside the earthier and more substantial mystery of the Great Mother, *Gaia*, and Her presence, too, in all things. Together, God and Gaia dictated the cycle of the seasons, the flow of the waters, the growth of the crops, the running of the fish in the sea and all the staples of nature on which the life of the village depended.

The longer I stayed in the village, the more I realized that it was the balance between spirit and nature that these people revered. The spirits, compelled to descend from their ethereal realm, entered into matter, giving substance and beauty and grace to the material world. Thus, the spirit knew its own eternity, and that sense of timelessness was reflected in the cycle of birth, growth, death and rebirth witnessed yearly in the harvest of nature's bounty and accepted as a vital part of the human condition. Uncontaminated by philosophical dualism, life here seemed to have no over-riding *philosophical meaning*, only the purpose of giving expression to the spirit-matter interface, holding the tension that drew the world of the spirits and the world of nature together.

I soon grew comfortable with the sensation of time transcended and mysteriously cognizant of my immortal spirit's generations. My cultural heritage lay in the British Isles, but I knew that the lineage of my spirit went back in time and space to the Greeks. I felt so comfortable on this island that I could imagine that the lineage of my spirit knew Crete well. If so, then an ancient incarnation of my spirit had belonged to the Earth Mother goddess long before it took up the sword and became a warrior spirit in service to the warlords of the patriarchy.

When I began to understand these things, I began painfully to understand what we had done in Vietnam. There was little difference between the peasants of Vietnam and the peasants of Crete. They both had a simplistic view of modern reality and a deep intuitive sense of how the spiritual essence permeated all things. When peasants in Crete prayed for rain, perhaps they did so in the church because it pleased the priest, but they cast their incantations to the winds so that God and Gaia could hear and bring the life-giving waters. When peasants in Vietnam cast their incantations to the winds, they were evoking the tears of Au Co that had been carried down into the palace of the Sea Dragon and turned into the nurturing rain that sustained their world.

Then we came to Vietnam, a mechanized army marching behind the god of death and bringing destruction to the peasant's world. We destroyed their homes, their villages, their crops, but our main objective was to destroy their connection to the Earth Mother goddess so that we could turn simple peasants into the workforce that produced the raw materials of an industrialized world, and turned that workforce into consumers of manufactured goods. The irony was that, from the peasant's point of view, the conflicting Titans that instigated the war both wanted the same thing. The *dialectical materialism* of communists and the *abject materialism* and *conspicuous consumerism* of capitalism both enslaved the soul and destroyed the peasant's deep reverence for the spirit-matter interface.

But then, everywhere the lives of simple people were under assault. Even Agia Galini—a timeless vortex inhabited by gnarled old peasants—was not immune to change, for their children and grandchildren now lived and worked in the urban culture of Heraklion—producing and consuming manufactured goods.

If indeed I unconsciously played a role in the subjugation of the Earth Mother, if that was the inclination that had carried my warrior spirit down through the long corridor of time and into the war in Vietnam, then I was ready to repent and change the purpose of my life. Consumed by the god of death and driven by the god of war to destroy, ravish and violate the goddess, my warrior spirit was now awake, cognizant of its own culpability and ready to repent.

Perhaps, the old people of the village knew of the crime I had committed against their divine parent. Perhaps they could read the deep sense of guilt that now emanated from the spirit-essence of my being. Perhaps they understood that, already, I had made this long journey in hopes of redeeming grace from the one who ruled hand-in-hand with the Father. Perhaps they watched with compassion the battle that still raged within me. But I also sensed that they did not judge me. Rather, their acceptance gave me a renewed feeling of a deep spiritual communion with all humanity. They would sit in the audience. Their dark eyes would bear witness to the dramatic redemption of my soul that—driven by instinct and intuition—I had come to Crete to find.

CHAPTER TEN:

Myrtos

After several more days in the village, I was relaxed enough to be friendly with some of the other tourists. Having decided to stay, I moved out of the old peasant woman's home and into a hotel room. I still shied away from the Americans, but I made friends with some Germans and with a young Israeli girl named Misha, whose mother had brought her to Greece to keep her from being drafted into the Israeli army. She was a tomboy, about seventeen, with long black hair and sabra eyes. When she saw me on the beach, she was bold and indiscreet in questioning me about the burn scars on my legs. When I told her that I had been in the war in Vietnam, she attached herself to me and prodded incessantly for stories about my war adventures. Perhaps her mother had sensed the Amazonian warrior spirit in her daughter and was doing her best to keep her child away from the ravages of war.

We often met in the evening, sitting together at one of the restaurants on the town square for the evening meal and wiling away leisurely hours with teasing conversation and flirtations kept innocent by the presence of Misha's mother. It was one of those concessions to normalcy that made me feel at peace in Agia Galini, just as I had found a momentary respite from the war in that peasant village in Vietnam, and so I was at peace with the world. But after I had been there for about ten days, all that tranquility was shattered by two new arrivals.

☆ ☆ ☆

I had been walking on the path above the cliffs to the west. There, not far from the village, the southern slope of Mount Ida rose sharply upward. A shepherd with a dog herded the white undulating body of his flock over a dark green meadow of spring grasses that covered the gentle slope between the sea cliffs and the scattered stands of pine that stood guard at the base of a sharp upheaval of granite. Below the path, a rugged wall of sandstone plunged two hundred feet to the waves that splashed against the rocks. I walked about a mile and a half to a steep gully that ran down the side of the mountain and into the sea. Then, I turned back.

Sunset was approaching. In the western sky the sun had become a fiery red ball that glowed through a haze that shimmered in waves of pink and gold. The sky above was an unbroken dome of blue in which the full, white orb of the moon had risen in the east to co-rule the sky before pushing the sun from a heaven impatient for night. The sea, no longer sparkling in the sunlight, was a quiet plane of aquamarine upon the face of the deep. As I walked back toward the village, the peaceful feeling that I had accumulated in the past few days resonated deep within me.

Then suddenly, the muscles and sinews of my body began to pulse with an unfamiliar and uncontrollable excitement. A mystic aura preceding a meeting of souls, a spirit force of great power, grabbed my heart and pulled me rapidly toward its source. My heart pounded in my chest awakening my Eros spirit, which leapt from my breast and dragged my body along at a blinding pace. Never before had the spiritual essence of another affected me so powerfully.

As I mounted a rise that looked down on the village square, I saw them. A warm, moist wind blew up from the sea and caressed the nape of my neck, sending shivers down my spine. The two youths, their backpacks displaying the faded red maple leaf of the Canadian flag, were speaking with Misha, whose gestures and animation revealed that a passionate vibration had touched her as well. I tried to hide the palpitations of my heart as I descended to the plaza and introduced myself.

These new arrivals—university students from Toronto—were handsome, slender youths with an androgynous look that was prevalent at that time and which I found very attractive. Lane had shoulder-length brown hair that flowed softly and twirled when it caught the wind. His penetrating eyes were not the usual crystal blue, but the color of the deep blue sea. He looked at me with a sharp look, a faint smile and a nod, then turned back to continue his animated conversation with Misha. Lane kept her captivated, holding intense eye contact with her, speaking with a smooth flirtatious seduction and a powerful sensuality in all his gestures. Her face glowed. The attraction between them was evident.

The other boy, Steven, had blond hair that also tumbled to his shoulders, soft and clean like unwoven threads of silk. I could not take my eyes off him, for he was the source of the passionate spirit that had clutched my heart and drawn me to him. He did not look directly at me, but watched his friend. Was he embarrassed by my stare? Did he also feel the powerful erotic energy that seemed to flow right through me and was directed at him? It threw me off balance, and I could think of nothing to say.

Then, as though he felt my eyes caressing him he turned and looked directly at me. His soul gazed out at me through the jade-green circles of his eyes. Once more my heart leapt out of my chest, and a mysterious spark of energy arched across the space between us, electrifying the already tensely charged atmosphere. Misha felt that spark, stumbled on her words and shifted her eyes nervously between our faces.

Lanes soft lips curled his hairless cheeks into a smile, and he looked knowingly at me. Then he draped his arm possessively over his friend's shoulder, as if to protect him from an unwelcomed suitor. Then he turned and continued his conversation with Misha. I did not know how to react and fought to stay calm. As it was, I was feeling like an intruder, barging in on a conversation between a girl and a boy exploring their mutual attraction. Steven, soft-spoken and shy, turned his eyes back to the ground and remained passively silent. Perhaps he did not want to intrude on Lane's seduction, but neither did he acknowledge my attraction to him—an attraction that must have been evident.

Trying to change the ambiance and recover some of my own composure, I suggested that we all go to Cleo's for something to drink. We talked and drank coffee until the twilight shadows descended on the village. Lights came on in the restaurants and the tables began to fill for the evening meal. Misha informed us that an American couple that had been in Agia Galini for some time was leaving town. There would be a going-away party in their hotel room that night and everyone was invited. Lane said that they were going to the beach to find a camping site by the stream before the lingering twilight faded, but once they had set up their tent they would come to the party. I decided that I would go as well and returned to my hotel room with my emotions churning in turmoil.

I lay on my bed with my hands behind my head staring hypnotically at the ceiling fan. At first, I tried to tell myself that it was only infatuation. But no, that wasn't it at all. I had been severely wounded by the maddening poison on the tip of Cupid's arrow, and I was struck—as much as anyone could be struck—with love-at-first-sight. My Eros spirit had lain dormant for so long—buried under the weight of my mother's death, intimidated by my father's expectations and drowned by Thanatos— that its sudden awakening, in the form of a mysterious and powerful homoerotic passion that was still forbidden by modern society, threw me completely off balance. I tried to focus on a plan to break through Steven's defenses and on defining what I wanted for the night ahead. Did the androgynous look that had become popular while I was in the army also mean that he might be open to sexual experimentation? For the answer to that question I would have to rely on spontaneous inspiration. I jumped from my bed, took a cold shower to quell the flames in my loins and dressed for an evening out.

The party was held in a large, second-floor hotel room with whitewashed walls and lit by a symphony of candles placed on tables, windowsills and in odd nooks and crannies in the walls. It was a warmly decorated room with beds and chairs covered in brightly colored, handwoven shawls and blankets of red, blue, yellow, purple and green collected by the couple over several months. They were familiar local figures and knew nearly all of the foreign tourists in town who now crowded into the room and spilled out onto the staircase that climbed up the outside wall of the small hotel. I felt a bit out of place because I had purposely avoided so many of those people, including the hosts. Regardless of the high ideals that made me unsociable, I realized that some of them probably perceived me as a snob. It was embarrassing. I drank Retsina, hoping that the bitter wine would loosen me up, dissolve my uneasiness and break down some of the barriers of my shyness. I spoke politely to people I had seen in the plaza and on the beach.

Then, when the muse of civil conversation failed me, I quietly moved toward the window balcony that looked down on the street, where I could watch for Steven and Lane.

They came late, dressed in clean clothes that were wrinkled from having been stuffed in their backpacks. Lane wore a blue scarf around his neck that accented the sparkle in his blue eyes. Steven, wore a cream-colored shirt that accented his tan and, like mine, was open to the forth button in the fashion of young Italians. He wore a jade-green pendant on a leather thong around his neck. I watched the flicker of candlelight on their faces as the entered the room, accepted glasses of wine from our hosts and introduced themselves congenially to strangers.

Not surprisingly, Lane was the more socially gregarious of the two. Steven stood shyly, passively, by his side while Lane, his arm around Misha, captivated an audience with the animation and gaiety of his conversation. I waited nervously for a sign of recognition. Then Steven lifted his eyes and scanned the room. Once more, his eyes met mine with a powerful spark. This time, there was no mistaking the powerful erotic energy that passed between us. He too must have been embarrassed by the spark that could have electrified the whole room but was probably only registered by others as an odd blip added to the otherwise normal social vibration. We each turned, quickly, to talk with other guests. My heart was beating uncontrollably in my chest. My nerves were tense. Then, after an eternity of silence, Steven drifted away from Lane and came toward the balcony. My palms sweated.

"Hi. I'm glad you came...I mean, glad you guys came to the party." My voice was broken and nervous.

"Yeah," was all he said. He didn't really smile, though for a moment he looked into my eyes and held out his hand. I took it with a soft shake, savoring the feeling of his palm brushing mine—a light touch that rushed through the sinews of my body making the torch in my heart glow a little brighter. Then, without another word, he turned to look out the window at the quiet village. His mood turned inward, as though he pulled a veil over his thoughts and feelings, shutting me out. I wondered if he was waiting, passively, for me to start the conversation, but I was too mesmerized and just stared at him, as I had done in the plaza, earlier in the evening.

In the flicker of the candlelight, his hair turned to a soft, golden glow. His cheeks were smooth and virginal, and his full lips, moistened by the wine, glistened in the dim light. His cotton shirt hung limply from his shoulders and carried the sweet scent of his body that blossomed in the moist heat of the room. I watched as a bead of perspiration trickled down the side of his neck, across his collarbone and spread as a light sheen over the tan muscles of his chest. When I thought I detected a glimmer in the corner of his eye, I touched his elbow. He stiffened. My heart beat more wildly. I tried to speak, but feeling a preemptive sting of rejection, my voice cracked. I could think of nothing to say. Damn! Had I learned nothing about seduction from Rudi?

My words, which should have expressed a soft and eloquent flow of my passions, fell flat and turned against me, suffocating my own fire and drowning the one I had hoped to ignite. Steven's mood didn't help. When he turned inward, his shyness and passivity became defensive barriers through which I could not break.

Lane came to the balcony, still bubbling with swashbuckling exuberance. Perhaps he was trying to rescue his friend. We talked, for Lane was easy to talk to. Yet each time I looked back at Steven my soul leapt from the cavity in my breast, and the mysterious light of the Eros spirit mesmerized my conscious mind. When Misha joined us, the mood shifted once again, and it seemed as though we were back to where we had started the evening in the plaza with Steven staring at the floor, Lane flirting with Misha and me standing on the sidelines.

After the party, alone in my room, I tried to understand the failure of my seduction. I wanted to believe that this powerful erotic passion was mutual. If that was the case, I didn't understand why we couldn't turn a spontaneous soulful attraction into a night of making love. But if he had felt that power as an overwhelming force, then perhaps the intensity had frightened him. Certainly, it frightened me. Maybe the following day I would be more successful. Through great agitation and discomfort, I slept.

The next morning, after a light breakfast in the plaza, I headed for the beach. The fire of my passion still smoldered, but I was more in control of my emotions. From where I placed my towel, I could see their campsite, but instead of approaching I just watched from a distance, waiting for them to emerge from their tent. When they finally came to the beach, we greeted each other casually, erasing, I hoped, the night-marish memory of the night before. They dropped their towels beside me and walked into the water.

I could not take my eyes off of them. Lane was slender with tight muscles on his chest and abs that descended in graceful ripples into his low-slung swimming trunks. Steven, though his personality was softer than Lane's hard-edged extroversion, was actually more muscular, with a physique like a young Apollo and a dark tan accented by his fine, sun-bleached hair. I watched them splash and play, dark and mysterious figures against the brightly shining waters of a calm morning sea.

I made no attempt to disguise the homoerotic feelings that had made me uncomfortable in the States but with which I had become more comfortable with Rudi. Though in Greece those feelings seemed natural, I knew that I had a lot to learn about how to direct them, for they were spiritual as well as physical. As I watched the two boys, clas-sic Hellenic images took hold in my imagination. I saw Hermes and Apollo playing together in the water—strong, powerful embodiments of masculine perfection. Their handsome faces, framed with soft curls, possessed that kind of androgynous beauty that belonged to the gods, defied time and radiated from the spirits dancing in their souls. But too, boys will be boys. I had already detected the devilish mischievousness of Hermes that lay behind Lane's veil of sensuality. Steven's true nature was more hidden and defensive. Not even Dionysus could have easily seduced the controlled nature of that young Apollo. My vision of two young gods strengthened my conviction that my passion was weighted with the responsibility *not* to violate the sacredness of a divine spirit with an aggressive seduction.

I had encountered aggressive seductions from gays in New Orleans and in Munich, and I did not like it. When I met gays who were hus-tling, I found them insensitive and just out looking for sex. In a world dominated by straight men, most gays remained closeted, so that in the closed circle of the gay community casual sex was accepted and often solicited in an atmosphere where aggression and outrageous behavior were the norms, part of the game.

But from Rudi I had learned that homoeroticism, too, could be treated with great sensitivity. That was the way that Rudi had treated me, speaking softly to my soul, making sure that my Eros spirit was listening to him and that our desire was mutual before broaching the subject of sex. I, too, wanted to lay upon the couch of love with another who touched my soul.

The boys came out of the sea, laughing and frolicking in the sand and sat down beside me. Fortunately, my insane passion of the night before had dissipated and we could talk normally. Lane was curious about the scars on my legs, and I told him about being in the Vietnam War.

That riled him. Lane shot off on a passionate and long-winded dissertation in opposition to the war, justifying the social unrest it caused, not only on college campuses in the United States, but on the campus of their own university in Canada. While Lane overwhelmed the conversation, Steven withdrew into a moody, introverted silence. His moodiness was mysterious and, ironically, it was that mystery that I found so attractive—as though it was a perfect reflection of the unknown mystery of my own soul. Slowly, my attention drifted away from Lane's tiresome exuberance, and once more I caressed Steven with my eyes. He revived my Eros spirit—the spirit that had been distorted by the killer instinct and now longed, desperately, to commune with the soul of this Canadian boy with long golden hair.

When the evening came, soft as a whisper, I saw Lane in the plaza talking with Misha, but I found Steven alone at the end of the seawall skipping stones on the glassy smooth surface of the sea. I threw a stone that skipped across the rings made by his. He looked up at me in silence and his gaze beckoned me to sit beside him. I talked, holding back my passion, though it twisted knots in my stomach. I was only trying to keep my words flowing smoothly and calmly, hoping that my heart would take charge of my speech, fire my words with love and tenderness and ignite the spark of love in his heart.

I felt him soften, just a little, and a shy smile lit his face. For the first time since we had met, Steven's true personality—no longer overwhelmed by Lane's exuberance or intimidated by my projection—began to show. He was quiet and deeply sensitive. I sensed that shyness was his defense against the deep feelings that could easily overwhelm him when confronted with new and unfamiliar experiences. Steven reawakened in me the sensitivity that I had felt with Mike, before our military training turned our passions cold, honed to the instinct of survival in the war. In the military, I had learned to bury that sensitivity behind a mask of false bravado. If Steven perceived me as a threat, perhaps it came from the false bravado that still distorted my sensitivities.

Those sensitivities could more easily be expressed with a touch than with words, and I touched Steven's forehead with my finger and lifted a lock of his hair away from his face. We looked into each other's eyes for a moment. "You are so beautiful," I said. Then I stumbled with embarrassment with the words that had fallen so unexpectedly out of my lips. Fearful that I had overstepped some line with Steven, I tried to backtrack. "Of course beauty is in the eye of the beholder...but...I mean...beauty like a guy; not like a girl...of course."

He didn't run away. Rather, a smile lit his face and he laughed gently at my awkward flattery. For a moment, I was certain that I had touched something inside him and my passion glowed, once more. I wanted to kiss him. Perhaps, my unspoken vision flashed too readily from my eyes to his imagination—a telepathic communion between souls. He said that he should be going back to town and stood to leave.

Together we walked back to the village and joined Lane and Misha at Cleo's.

The four of us drank ouzo and conversed with a much smoother rapport than when we had met twenty-four hours earlier. Steven emerged from his shell to display a boyish immaturity. I sensed that he was, indeed, a delicate youth who might still have been a virgin. That would explain his shyness and why he was so defensive. But, after that moment on the seawall, I also sensed that he knew I could be gentle with him. And so there was hope.

That night, I slept more calmly, partly because I had been exhausted by the emotional turmoil of the past twenty-four hours, but also because I was beginning to believe that in another day or two the powerful attraction that I wanted so desperately to believe was mutual might find resolution and that we might both surrender to the power of our sexual desire.

Early the following morning when I went for my usual breakfast in the plaza, I met Lane. He was wearing his backpack and Steven was not in sight. A crowd of people had gathered, as usual, near the morning bus that stood in the plaza, receiving passengers for the trip back to Heraklion. Steven had already boarded the bus. When I saw him in the window, our eyes met briefly, then he turned away. I was too stunned by the situation to react, for I had simply assumed that they would join the tourist population of Agia Galini as I had done. Lane told me that they were returning to the small fishing village where they had left their Volkswagen van with friends. He also told me that they would be staying there for some time. When I asked, he told me how to get to Myrtos. Then he said goodbye.

I was still stunned as I watched the bus pull away, pass the church and climb the hill on the road back to Heraklion. A warm, moist wind swelled up from the sea and tickled the hairs on the nape of my neck. I had, after all, come to Crete to surrender myself to the mystic wind. Was this a part of how the mystery of healing my soul was going to play itself out? As the morning dragged on, my heart grew heavy with the sadness of not even having had a chance to speak with Steven or say goodbye. Yet something in his eyes had beckoned me, or so I thought. By the afternoon I was a neurotic mess. The mystery was not yet resolved. The drama was not yet over.

All my instincts told me that a part of me had departed with Steven— that whatever I had projected onto him out of my soul had gotten on that bus and disappeared. Now it was not just that I wanted to find him—wanted some satisfactory conclusion to the spark that had ignited between us—I had to find him. I had to chase-after that mysterious, unknown Eros spirit that Steven had awakened and then taken away with him. The entire experience had been surrealistic—a cosmic drama with an unknown director. For example Lane, with a devilish sparkle in his eye, had played his part too, for he had been very clear with his instructions on how to get to Myrtos.

I left Agia Galini on the afternoon bus.

☆ ☆ ☆

The journey to Myrtos was not an easy trip. I crossed the island, arriving in Heraklion in the evening and had to spend the night there. The following day, I took a bus that followed the north coast east to Agios Nikolaos, changed buses again and re-crossed the island to the town of Ierapetra. There, too, I arrived so late in the afternoon that I had to spend the night. Though Myrtos was only ten kilometers away, the only direct route was a rugged footpath along the coast, too dangerous to navigate in the dark even if one wanted to walk the distance. The only bus left at five in the morning and wound through several mountain villages before arriving, three hours later, in Myrtos—a tiny fishing village beneath the southern slope of Mount Dikti.

Myrtos was not a tourist destination, and it was not inviting. There were no hotels or restaurants. Where the bus stopped, there was only a cluster of small, concrete houses gathered together near a black sand beach at the edge of the sea. Behind the village the mountain rose, not as gentle terraces of olive trees, but over naked hills, which angled sharply, 7,000 feet up a steep slope to the snowcapped peak. Though the air was warm, it was thick and heavy in the early morning, and gray clouds hung low over the sea. They blocked the disk of the rising sun and quickly gathered around the trunk of the mountain. I was fatigued by my three-day journey and the powerful emotions brought about by the irrational resolve that drew me to Myrtos. The dreariness of the day, which promised nothing but drizzle, deepened the shadows over the landscape and darkened the veil that was drawn across my mind.

My logical decision-making processes had been thrown out of control, usurped by the erotic, irrational passions that boiled in my soul. A powerful and illogical stream of images clashed and tumbled through my mind with frightening speed, mixing and mingling the faces of the people I had met—Steven, Lane, Misha, the old peasant woman, the gnarled old men and women of Agia Galini—with the history and mythology of this island in the middle of the wine-dark sea. Nothing made sense. There was no consistency to the images and no logic or reason to my actions. I had entered the mystic realm of my own volition, but now I was at the mercy of embroiled emotions that pulled me this way and that, forcing me to reach deep inside and hold tight to whatever meaning I could find in the disheveled pile of my feelings and my intuition. Though I did not know where this journey was leading, I sensed that it was directed by some unseen deity that drew me ever deeper into the labyrinthine corridors of the landscape of my soul. Like Prince Theseus in the labyrinth of the Minotaur, I unraveled the thread of my knotted ball of sanity behind me, hoping that it would lead me out again.

It was the light of Eros that shone in Steven that drew me into the labyrinth, and he assumed a dimension far greater than a soul I wanted to commune with and a body I wanted to touch. He had become the living symbol of *my* Eros spirit. Only once before—when I was with Rudi—had the light of Eros shown so brightly through the dark shadows that, for many years, had enveloped my soul. As strange as this adventure had become, I sensed that it was the right pathway toward healing the conflict between love and death that still clashed in my soul and frustrated my initiation into selfhood.

I walked down onto the black sand beach toward a group of three or four vans parked together, several hundred yards beyond the concrete houses. Steven and Lane sat on a blanket on the sand along with five or six other young people. Lane looked at me with an insincere grin rather than a welcoming smile, while Steven acted completely indifferent. The sudden impression that the whole group was just a band of hippies cast Lane and Steven in a completely different light than the two young Canadian students they had seemed when I had first met them in Agia Galini. This new impression came as a complete shock, making me even more uncomfortable.

It was not that I disliked hippies. My contact with that loose, self-definition of young people had been limited to brief encounters in Munich and New Orleans, but I really didn't know any. My overall impression was that, while I was becoming a responsible and self-disciplined officer in the United States army, the hippies were going in the other direction—away from responsibility and self-discipline, characterized by the choice to passively, *"go with the flow," "hang loose"* and *"do-your-own-thing."* I, too, was looking for a new direction to transform my life. I had surrendered to the mystic realm by opening myself to my imagination, intuition and feelings, but I did not use drugs to get there. It seemed to me that hard-core hippies surrendered themselves completely to the mystical experience under the influence of drugs. I already knew there were powerful forces there that we could not understand, and they could make you crazy. Some of the hippies I had met were crazy. But too, there were many young people on the fringes who were just stepping cautiously into the mysterious realm of the soul, and they too used drugs. Like me, they did not want to lose their way back to objective reality, but the fact that they used drugs to enter the mystic realm and I did not made me irrationally judgmental of them.

Both Steven and Lane, who probably fell into that category, were completely different than they had been just three days before. Lane, whose exuberant, extroverted personality had enraptured the whole colony of tourists in Agia Galini in a flash, now sat in a quiet, lulled stupor. Steven seemed more introverted and withdrawn than ever. The others in the small group were no more animated.

Finally, someone asked me to sit. As we talked, I observed every-one—feeling out the relationships and the dynamics of the group. After a few minutes, my attention became focused on a young Canadian or American who sat directly across the blanket from me and was intro-duced as Spirou.

He was thin, almost to the point of emaciation, with long, stringy hair, a scraggly beard and deep-set dark eyes that seemed far too intense for a young face. His pallid skin, drawn tightly around the wide sock-ets of his eyes and over his prominent cheekbones, gave his features a sharpness that was disturbing. When he realized that my attention was focused on him, he grinned, pulling back his thin lips over stained, uneven teeth that gave him a sinister look. He was younger than me—perhaps twenty-two or twenty-three—but a bit older than the others. He had been living in Myrtos for several months in a house that he rented from one of the villagers, and he had taken a Greek name.

It didn't take long for me to realize that Spirou had a powerful influ-ence over the small group, which included another boy and several young women, all about the same age as Lane and Steven. Unlike Misha in Agia Galini, these girls were neither physically attractive nor vibrant, and I wondered why Lane and Steven had been attracted to this small commune led by a ragged guru. At least, it appeared to me that Spirou was some sort of so-called "spiritual" leader. I sensed that he projected his intensity and power out of the same mystic realm where I was treading ever so lightly. I also sensed that within the mystic realm Spirou and I were opposing spirits. We both knew it. Steven—whom I longed for and who carried the projection of my Eros spirit—was clearly under Spirou's influence. In the mystic realm, that put Steven right in the middle between us.

I did not know how Spirou had come to hold such power over the group, but the abrupt change of personality, particularly in Lane, made me suspect that drugs were the primary mechanism of control. Spirou's influence over Steven indirectly affected me, for it meant that my projected Eros spirit was held captive to his power. Sitting there with them made me feel uncomfortable and vulnerable. Though I did not have the impression that Spirou knew anything about the irrational, erotic obsession that had drawn me to Myrtos, I thought it best to withdraw. I left my gear with them and wondered down the beach to a quite place by some rocks where I could swim, try to relax the nervous tension that flowed through my mind and body, and think about what was happening to me.

In the late afternoon the intermittent drizzle turned to a steady rain and the air became thick with a chilling fog. Having nowhere else to go, I took shelter in the boys' van, along with several others from the group. Steven and Lane were livelier than they had been in the early morning, though Lane did not regain his exuberance. Steven played the guitar while everyone huddled close and fondled each other in fraternal intimacy. Spirou ducked, energetically, in and out of the van while other hippies, whom I had not met, came and went all afternoon. There seemed to be a *buzz* of activity around the camp, initiated by Spirou, and this intuition made me suspicious. I sensed that he was up to something, for I considered it probable that while I was swimming either Steven or Lane—probably Lane—had shared the story of what had transpired in Agia Galini, revealing my erotic obsession with Steven.

Inside the van, I could feel rejection from the others, but it only bothered me in so far as it affected my relationship with the boys. Lane and I talked, but Steven, who seemed to be as sensitive to feeling-toned impressions as I was, remained withdrawn, plucking his guitar. Each time Spirou ducked his head into the van he looked at me with his intense eyes and grinned a sinister grin but said nothing. Despite my discomfort, we spent a lazy, rainy afternoon together. I was trying to *hang-loose,* waiting to see what was going to happen next. There was no place else to stay and no way to leave Myrtos, except to walk back to Ierapetra in the rain, so I had become a reluctant captive of that small band of hippies.

When night came creeping through the drizzle and the fog, we moved to Spirou's house. The group mysteriously increased to about fifteen young people, including a contingent of Germans led by a good looking young man who spoke English. Another German was a large young man with a full red beard. Also, there were several young German women.

Some of the women prepared food. I had little choice but to go-with-the-flow, even though it made me feel aimlessly passive. Then, Steven began to play some familiar songs on his guitar, and everyone sang.

After the meal I sat talking with Steven. There was no false bravado in my voice, and I spoke softly while he plucked his guitar, practicing chords. I told him how impressed I was with his playing and tried to find the words that would make him smile again, for I wanted to feel the soft flash I had seen in his eyes that evening on the seawall in Agia Galini. He did not smile. His eyes did not flash. When Spirou called to him, he stood abruptly and went. I took that opportunity to relieve myself in the backyard of the house, for there was no bathroom.

When I returned to the room, they were gone. On cue from Spirou, his group had run laughing to the beach. Those damned hippies had been toying with me all afternoon, and it was Spirou's game. I did not understand his motives, but I did know that he appeared to maintain a powerful control over his group and that his motives were not innocent. Perhaps he felt that I was a threat to his control games. Or perhaps my vulnerability was too visible, so I bore the brunt of an afternoon's diversion. Still, my heart sank like a stone, for I had been foolish in leaving my feelings so open and vulnerable. What hurt me the most was the feeling that my own Eros spirit had rejected me.

I had no choice but to spend the night in the house with several others, including the big German with the red beard who snored. I hid my feelings and my tears, but I could not dismiss Steven so easily. I had been caught in a web of passion and desire that was cruelly frustrated; my Eros spirit had been awakened and then deserted. Now all I could think about was searching the corridors of my inner labyrinth for the deity who hid in the dark, manipulating the shadow threads that played on my emotions and pulled me toward an, as yet, unrealized goal.

I lay in my sleeping bag that I had rolled out on the cold concrete floor. Slowly, the portals of my conscious mind closed, and I surrendered myself to sleep. But my spirit was far too agitated to succumb to the quietude of dreamlessness. Mysterious dreams and symbols flew through the dark corridors of my mind, and a vivid dream preceded my waking. In this dream I witnessed a brilliant pageant that could have marched off of the frescoed walls of the palace of Knossos, combining the events of my experience with the magical, mythical proto-history of Crete.

The pageant was marching toward me, and it was led by a beautiful youth with long, flowing hair. He wore a loincloth of white linen tied around his slender waist with a wide belt of royal blue. There were bracelets of red and blue enamel on his wrists, and on his head was a golden crown with three ostrich plumes flowing from it. In his hand he held a rope attached to the nose-ring of a bull, huge and fully mature, that walked dutifully behind him. He walked, as though in a trance, between throngs of people who cheered and sang and played on flutes and drums.

The pageant arrived in a plaza. There was a round altar stone in the center where a priest with dark eyes and long stringy hair stood with a knife in each hand raised to catch the glint of the sun. Suddenly, the flutes and drums stopped. There was silence in the air, and the people held their breath anticipating the moment when She would reveal herself.

From the portal of a house at the edge of the plaza a woman appeared quite suddenly. Her steps were so light that she seemed to float out of the doorway and across the paving stones of the plaza. She wore a long dress that fell in seven layers to her bare feet. It had long sleeves, but the bodice was open to expose her full, round, naked breasts. In her hands, she held two serpents that wound themselves around her arms, and on her head was a crown of gilded, polished bull's horns supporting a golden disk between them that represented the sun. As She floated into the plaza, She began to move in a slow, rhythmic, hypnotic dance to the beat of a lone drum.

The bull was led to the altar. She blessed the animal. When its head had been lowered to the altar stone, the knives of the priest slashed through the air and blood flowed from the open wound in the neck of the dying bull. The blood was gathered in goblets and the priest, kneeling before Her, offered it up for the blessing of the goddess. Ceremonially, the blood was carried into a field and poured out as a libation upon the ground—a sacrifice to nurture the harvest of the grain for the following year.

All returned to the plaza. Then, without a word, the youth knelt before the goddess, received a blessing and moved to the altar stone. The priest, with his knives poised in the air, looked directly at me and grinned...

The sinister image jolted me awake. It was pitch black and silent in the room, with only the sound of the red-bearded German snoring. Outside a gentle rain beat down on the roof of the house and cool air swirled through the room, making me shiver. I realized that in my dream the youth was that of Steven and the priest was Spirou. But I knew that they really only represented forces within me—the spirits of Eros and Thanatos, the gods of love and death. However, the divinity who stood above them both was the Great Mother goddess, and I realized that it was She who had brought me to Myrtos, one of her most ancient and sacred sites, a mysterious locale of healing power.

She was the Goddess of the Corn, the Goddess of the Moon— the whispered voice of the night wind that had blown so percipiently through the open portals of my mind fourteen years before. She was all of the ancient goddesses—*Inanna* and *Ishtar* and *Isis* and *Cybele*— who, in the primordial past, had come to Crete. Though Her names are known, Her image and power have been all but forgotten. Yet She is the ancient deity of warfare *and* motherhood, of destruction *and* nurture. She commands all the phases of the life cycle: birth and growth, love and death and rebirth. That gives her license to be both chaste and promiscuous, a nurturer of newborn infants and bloodthirsty for meaningful sacrifice. The goddess presides over life and over the gods of love and death.

As man is born of woman, Eros and Thanatos are the twin gods born of the Great Mother goddess. Both reside in our immortal souls. What flooded over me was a divine revelation of transformation: that having confronted both my Thanatos and Eros spirits, I was free to choose to serve either Love or Death. When turned into a mechanized soldier, the warrior is only interested in the destruction of the enemy and serves the god of death. But the transformation of the warrior into serving the Eros spirit is the objective of the heroic struggle in the soul between love and death.

Then I understood the monster in the labyrinth—the Titans released from Tartarus—that spread over the world like a dark cloud without limits, ruling not just over death on the field of battle, but over pestilence and illness, over wanton slaughter and greed and the destruction of the balance in nature. The monster could dominate love, perverting the Eros spirit into an agent of lust and control.

Now, having finally seen the Great Mother goddess, the presence I had so powerfully sensed in the Illinois cornfield of my childhood, I no longer belonged to the warlords of the patriarchy. Having seen Her in my dream She reclaimed me as an age-old son of the mother, and serving Her was my alternative to serving the patriarchy. Already, She had manipulated the mysterious shadow threads in the corridors of my soul, fired my erotic passions, coerced the Eros spirit to awaken within me and led me down to Myrtos.

But none of the adventure absolved me of my guilt, absolved my warrior spirit that had participated in a war, perhaps in millennia of wars, against the Great Mother goddess. Because my guilt—my crimes— were as yet unresolved, the Great Mother goddess seemed to me a harsh and demanding judge, frightening to look upon. Still, She had not condemned and destroyed me but only had warned me in that dream that the god of death had the power to destroy my Eros spirit. My initiation into selfhood was not complete. I had only reached the first doorway—the doorway into the realm of the Mother.

I left Myrtos on the morning bus. I had hoped, somehow, that Steven and Lane would come up to the village that morning, for I could not bring myself to go look for them on the beach. They did not. The purpose of our brief encounter had been achieved and, though it left a bleeding wound in my heart, the pain of that wound reminded me that my heart was open. There, on a black sand beach in Crete, in the shadow of a dead volcano, abandoned by a blond boy who was, at once, the acolyte of a dark guru and the personified projection of my Eros spirit, I arrived at a highly improbable rebirth. I knew that from that moment on, my life would be transformed.

✦ ✦ ✦

The trip back to Heraklion was unsettling. My unrequited desire for Steven tore me apart, and it took all of my will power to continue the journey, changing buses in Ierapetra and again in Agios Nikolaos. Each leg of the journey became a twisted battle in my mind between turning back toward the source of all my pain and fleeing from it. By the time I stepped off the bus in Heraklion, I was exhausted from the battle with myself. It was already evening, but I had made up my mind to leave, that very night, on the ship back to Piraeus. Somehow, I would pull myself together, return to the states where I could find a job for the rest of the summer and complete the paperwork for my GI Bill. I would move forward with my plan to study philosophy at the London School of Economics in the fall, find sanctuary in the halls of academia and submerge myself in an adventure of the mind, far from the corridors of the mystic realm.

I went directly to the pier. At the ticket office I was told that there were no tickets left and that I would have to purchase one for the next boat that would leave on the following day. I was shocked. After puzzling over this new turn of events for a long, impatient moment, I bought a ticket for the next boat. Still, just the thought of having to find a hotel room for the night nearly overpowered the delicate forces that were holding my emotions and my sanity together.

Then, as I turned from the ticket window to leave the shipping office, I saw her. She was looking in my direction, though not at me, but there was no mistaking the familiar Scandinavian features, the short-cropped blond hair and the freckles across her nose that had not changed in five years. "Casey," I called out, knowing instantly the girl who had been Carl's girlfriend during the summer we spent at Spider Lake in Northern Wisconsin in 1966, before I enlisted in the army and a lifetime ago.

It only took a minute for her to recognize me, too. She was at the pier to say goodbye to a friend who was leaving after a short visit. When the shock of the incongruous meeting wore off, we found a café where we could renew our acquaintance. Casey told me that, after a few years of college, she had met a guy who was in the Air Force. It was her chance to escape from a rather closed life in Northern Wisconsin, and she moved in with him. When he was assigned to the American Air Force Base just outside Heraklion, she moved with him to Crete where they rented an apartment in town.

Casey asked me about Carl. I could only tell her that I knew he had been sent to Germany, but I did not know where. We had exchanged a few letters over the years, but gradually lost contact with each other.

When I asked her about her younger brother, Max, with whom I had formed a special bond that summer, she almost broke into tears. Max had graduated from high school and joined the Marines. A few months into his tour in Vietnam, he had stepped on a landmine. He wasn't killed, but he had lost a leg and was paralyzed in one arm. He had spent nearly a year in the hospital and was out now, but he was drinking heavily and taking drugs. Casey said that both she and her parents were trying to encourage him to go to college in the fall. I remembered the bright, good-looking kid that I had known during that peaceful summer, such a long time ago.

Casey invited me to spend the night in the apartment that she shared with her boyfriend, and I was happy not to have to go looking for a hotel room. It seemed such an incongruous coincidence, meeting Casey in Crete, and yet there are no coincidences. Every coincidence is really a synchronicity directed by mysterious, unseen forces. Meeting Casey took me back to that time just before I received my draft notice and joined the army—back into the life I had left behind. Our encounter had a soothing effect on the neurotic agitation that had resulted from my penetration of the mystic realm: the landscape of my soul. Perhaps it was a sign that I was making the right choice in returning to the states. Or was it a sign that I should stay in Europe?

More importantly, the meeting confirmed that I had finally gone through the transformation that took me beyond the Vietnam War. I had confronted the shadow in my own psyche represented by the god of death that lurks in all our souls and, though I had not vanquished him, I knew that I had it within myself to transform that power. I had made my confession before the Great Mother goddess who had guided me from the cornfields of Illinois to Myrtos, and I had begged Her for absolution for my sins against Her. I had also asked to know Eros, the god of love, as my inner guiding spirit, sensing that such knowledge would lead to the completion of my initiation into selfhood.

Ask, and you shall receive! I had only reached the first portal of initiation—guarded not by the warlords of the patriarchy after all, but by the Great Mother goddess. This conscious and very real confrontation with Her represented for me the profound mystery of my own soul. Its shimmering light could illuminate my life, but the soul also casts dark shadows that give the soul its depth. Paradoxically, it is by integrating the shadows of the soul that one finds the godhead and becomes illuminated. I had taken the first step, but the inward looking ego is only the beginning of the process. Now, the trials of my true initiation into selfhood could begin.

About the Author

When Mr. Mitchell reintegrated into American society, he taught secondary school for 27 years. He retired from teaching in 2006 after publishing his first book about education in America: NURTURING THE SOULS OF OUR CHILDREN: Education and the Culture of Democracy.